D1156446

THE INTERWAR YEARS

The Treaty of Versailles and the League of Nations

Ann Byers

Cavendish
Square
New York

Published in 2018 by Cavendish Square Publishing, LLC
243 5th Avenue, Suite 136, New York, NY 10016

Library of Congress Cataloging-in-Publication Data

Names: Byers, Ann, author.
Title: The Treaty of Versailles and the League of Nations / Ann Byers.
Description: New York : Cavendish Square Publishing, [2018] |
Series: The interwar years | Includes bibliographical references and index.
Identifiers: LCCN 2016053721 (print) | LCCN 2016054017 (ebook) |
ISBN 9781502627094 (library bound) | ISBN 9781502627100 (E-book)
Subjects: LCSH: Treaty of Versailles (1919) | League of Nations.
Classification: LCC D644 .B95 2018 (print) | LCC D644 (ebook) | DDC 940.3/141--dc23
LC record available at https://lccn.loc.gov/2016053721

Editorial Director: David McNamara
Editor: Kristen Susienka
Copy Editor: Alex Tessman
Associate Art Director: Amy Greenan
Designer: Alan Sliwinski
Production Coordinator: Karol Szymczuk
Photo Research: J8 Media

Printed in the United States of America

Contents

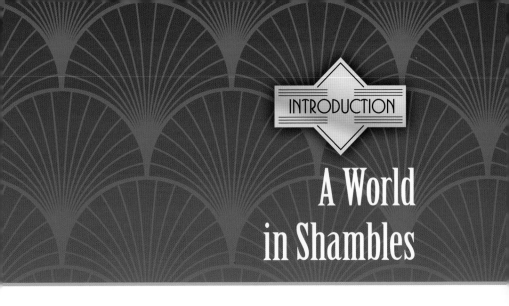

A World in Shambles

When the first global war ended in 1918, the world lay in ruins. Four years of fighting among the armed forces of thirty-two nations had wreaked unimaginable destruction throughout Europe, Asia, Africa, and into the Americas. No one had foreseen the length of the war or the extent of the damage, nor had anyone predicted the international disasters just ahead that would prolong the suffering.

The human toll alone was devastating. About 80 percent of the men of Germany and France between the ages of fifteen and fifty had gone to battle; more than two-thirds did not return. At least nine million soldiers were killed and twenty-one million were wounded. Civilian **casualties** were almost as high or higher. The number of deaths, military and civilian, attributed directly to the fighting was between fifteen and

Opposite: The town of Poelcapelle, Belgium, was leveled in October 1917 when British forces tried unsuccessfully to take it from the occupying German army.

After World War I, future US president Herbert Hoover directed America's relief mission bringing food to Europe. He is seen here bringing relief to Poland after World War II.

twenty million. A worldwide flu pandemic that began in the final year of the war added another fifty million to the total.

The physical destruction was almost equally disheartening. Throughout France, where much of the war was fought, the landscape was deeply pocked with bomb craters, trenches that once held soldiers, and miles of tunnels. Entire cities were leveled and towns and villages completely obliterated. Roads were gone, rail lines torn up, bridges demolished, and canals unusable. Three hundred thousand houses, fifteen hundred schools, and twelve hundred churches were totally destroyed.

The loss of people and property meant that economies were shattered. Germany, France, Russia, and other countries had lost huge numbers of farmers, tradesmen, and industrial workers. Many of those who came home found no jobs in the devastated cities. In France, six thousand factories had been crushed or gutted. Most of those that survived had been converted to war production and were not easily geared up again for peacetime use. Even if they could be retooled, the destruction of one hundred coal mines deprived them of fuel for operation. Agriculture was also difficult; more than 5 million acres (2 million hectares) of farmland was torn and scarred and 1.3 million livestock were dead. Both unemployment and starvation were very real specters haunting a demoralized Europe.

This map of Europe during World War I depicts the Central Powers (pink), the Allied Powers (green), and neutral countries (tan).

Governments and political systems were also in ruins. Four giant empires that had dominated Europe had collapsed. Ethnic populations within those empires clamored to form their own countries. Colonies in Africa and Asia rose up, demanding independence from their weakened European masters. The hardships of the war fueled a revolution that transformed Russia and ignited many smaller revolts across the continent. Mighty nations lost their grip and less influential countries flexed their muscles; the balance of power in the world had changed.

Power shifted within the various countries as well, playing havoc with social structures. When Europe went to war in

When men went to war, women—like this woman employed in an armaments factory—had to do the work at home. Working changed the social and economic positions of women.

1914, the soldiers and sailors—particularly the leaders—were largely from the upper classes. Serving in the military was considered an honor, and the educated and the privileged filled the ranks. As the war dragged on, the common people were drafted. Fighting and bleeding together in the muddy trenches united people of high and low status. After the war, the rich had lost their wealth and the commoners had gained a new confidence in their abilities. Poverty had leveled the social classes.

Never before had the world been so thoroughly broken. The shock and horror of the first large-scale war in a hundred years had shattered more than the landscape, the economy, and the political and social foundations. It had eaten away at the hearts and spirits of people. Disillusionment and distrust paralyzed many.

Could Europe be put back together? Homes and cities could be rebuilt. Forests and crops would eventually grow again. Enterprising people could start new businesses. But who would pay the enormous cost of reconstruction? Who *should* pay?

Everyone knew almost nothing would ever be the same. What should a new world look like? Where should the boundary lines be? What kinds of governments should the new countries have? What should happen to the colonies of the defeated nations? Could anything be done to ensure that such a terrible experience would never happen again? Most importantly, who should make all these decisions?

Conflicting Visions for Peace

The First World War officially stopped at 11 a.m. on November 11, 1918—the eleventh hour of the eleventh day of the eleventh month. The Central Powers—Austria-Hungary, Germany, Bulgaria, and the Ottoman Empire—had lost to the Allies. The Allies consisted of the Entente—mainly Great Britain, France, and Russia—and the United States as an Associated power.

Several months earlier, Russia and Romania, both Allies, had ceased fighting. They had signed treaties with the Central Powers, giving up large chunks of territory. The Central Powers appeared to be winning, but by the end of October, the tide had turned against them. The Ottoman and Austro-Hungarian Empires had begun to fall apart, and they made peace with the Allies. The Allied armies were advancing toward Germany. On November 11, Germany

Opposite: As the clock strikes 11 a.m. on November 11, 1918, citizens in London, England, wave British flags in celebration.

agreed to lay down its arms. Aboard a train car in the forest of Compiègne, France, representatives of Germany, France, and Britain signed the **armistice** that silenced the guns.

At Compiègne, Germany promised to stop its attacks only if and until a permanent peace arrangement could be worked out. The peace treaty would have to be acceptable to both the Allied countries and Germany. If it was not satisfactory, either side could resume the war. The armistice halted the fighting in November, but it took seven long months until the terms for peace were hammered out.

Allies' Visions for Peace

The Allied leaders were united in winning the war, but they did not agree on what should happen next. The three countries that had contributed the most to the Allied victory (with the exception of Russia, which was not involved with the German armistice) had different attitudes toward Germany. They had different national interests. Therefore, they had different ideas about how Germany should be treated.

Of all the countries in the war, France had suffered the greatest territorial devastation and the largest loss of life. France wanted revenge. A big part of that revenge was making Germany pay for all the damage the war had inflicted. France had another big interest: survival as a nation. Unlike the other Allies, France shared a long border with Germany as well as a history of conflict. The possibility that Germany might someday launch another strike, another war, terrified

The French statue titled Le Souvenir *(The Remembrance) depicts the provinces of Alsace and Lorraine as women, grief-stricken at their annexation by Germany in 1871.*

the French. Therefore, France wanted to strip Germany of everything it could use in a future war—its military might, its colonies, and as many of its economic resources as possible. In making peace, France's goal was to punish Germany and keep it weak.

Britain, too, had suffered great losses at the hand of Germany and also thought Germany should pay the bulk of the cost of rebuilding. However, Britain did not want to see its former enemy crushed as France did. Britain was a vast empire, geographically distant from Germany. Its main interests for the postwar period were economic. Germany had been and could once again become a trading partner. Britain wanted to see Germany regain its economic strength.

Britain had another reason for going more lightly than France on Germany. The country feared that an overly weak Germany would make Europe unstable. Toward the end of the war, a revolution had shaken Russia and a civil war was still going on there. The turmoil in Russia was beginning to spill into East Europe, and Britain hoped a somewhat strong Germany might be able to keep it from spreading. The only real threat a restored Germany posed to Britain was on the seas. Therefore, Britain's goal in making peace was to punish Germany some, but not too much, and limit its navy.

America's Vision

The third country with a voice in the war's aftermath was the United States. America had been late to enter the conflict. The mood of the country when war broke out was **isolationism**. People saw the war as a European affair, something happening "over there," and therefore not their business. The United States declared itself neutral and continued to maintain diplomatic relations and trade with all parties, particularly Britain.

However, when German submarines started sinking merchant ships with Americans aboard, the United States edged slowly away from neutrality toward the Allied cause. The final straw was the Zimmermann note, a telegram intercepted by British intelligence. In the coded message,

Germany tried to convince Mexico to declare war on the United States. America could no longer remain uncommitted. On April 6, 1917, the US Congress declared war on Germany, and the first small group of American troops arrived in France on June 26. The United States fought for fewer than seventeen months of the four-year war.

Unlike the European Allies, the United States had no territorial interests in the war's outcome. No battle was fought on American soil and no long-standing rivalries cried out for vengeance. All most Americans wanted was for the war to be over so they could resume their business dealings with London banks and European merchants.

US president Woodrow Wilson was originally just as isolationist as the rest of the country. He won reelection in 1916 with the slogan "He kept us out of war." Yet as the country found, neutrality grew harder and harder to maintain. Wilson needed to give the American public a reason for sending its soldiers "over there." The rationale he presented was not based on US self-interests. It was not about national security or self-defense or retaliation after the German submarine attacks. Wilson asked for a declaration of war on the grounds of a set of principles and ideals.

Wilson's Aims for War and Peace

Woodrow Wilson has been called an **idealist**. An idealist is governed by concepts or standards he thinks are right, even if the ideals are hard to reach. Wilson's main idea was that

Woodrow Wilson was president of Princeton University, then governor of New Jersey, then the twenty-eighth president of the United States (from 1913 to 1921).

the world must be made safe for democracy. His rationale for entering the war was to bring about peace. He was concerned not with national but international prosperity. His goal was not to gain anything for the United States, but to seek the good of all people in every country.

Shortly after declaring war, Wilson asked the Allies to state their war aims. What did they hope to gain if they were victorious? When no one responded, the president listed his own ideas in a speech to Congress on January 8, 1918. His idealism was evident in his use of words and phrases unusual in a war aims speech: "unselfish, impartial, good will, fair dealing." Wilson listed fourteen points for a "program of the world's peace." Following his program, Wilson said, would create a postwar world that would be "safe for every peace-loving nation." His Fourteen Points became the US vision for making peace.

The very first point called for the elimination of secret agreements between nations. Wilson felt that a web of secret alliances was an underlying cause of the war. Some of the nations of Europe had allied themselves with others— Germany with the Ottoman Empire, the Allies with Italy, and the Allies with Romania against Austria-Hungary. Some countries had made secret plans to carve up among themselves the territory of nations they hoped to defeat. Wilson believed countries should perform their negotiations and make pacts in public view. He thought transparency in international relations would stop or at least reduce plots and tensions.

NATIONS SEEK THEIR OWN COUNTRIES

Countries and nations are not the same thing. A geographic territory under a particular rule is a country or state. People with the same culture, language, and history are considered a nation or nationality. Sometimes a nation has its own country, but sometimes more than one nation lives in the same country.

In the late 1800s, three of the four great empires of Europe contained several nations. The Ottoman Empire was largely Turkish, but it included sizeable populations of Greeks, Armenians, Bulgarians, and others. The vast empire of Russia, although mainly Slavic, held many nationalities, including Romanians, Poles, Ukrainians, and Lithuanians. Austria-Hungary was even more complex, with thirteen different national groups. The nations were small parts of giant empires, but they were restless.

After the French Revolution (1787–1799) and throughout the nineteenth century, thoughts about liberty and equality spread throughout Europe. People without a voice in their own affairs began to believe they should and could govern themselves. Nations that had been crushed by larger or stronger powers felt they could blossom and thrive again. The ideas of freedom and equality gave hope to people who felt oppressed or ignored. People started to identify with their nationality rather than with their country or their king or emperor. **Nationalism** swept many ethnic communities of Europe.

The growing nationalism created tensions, at times erupting into violence. Friction was particularly strong in the Balkan peninsula of southeast Europe. The peninsula was strategically important, located at the crossroads between East and West and bordered by three major waterways. The Austro-Hungarian, Russian, and Ottoman Empires met in the Balkans.

The Balkan Peninsula was home to a great diversity of national groups, many increasingly yearning for their own countries. By 1913, with the

This is a recruitment poster for the Polish Army in France, in which thousands of Poles served. The flag and the soldier's armband feature the white eagle, a symbol for Poland.

Ottoman Empire unraveling, several nations had formed independent states, including Greece, Serbia, Bulgaria, and Albania. However, many people of those nationalities remained outside the territory of the new states, and nationalistic fervor stirred conflicts between the young countries and the neighboring empires. Intense nationalism was the spark that ignited World War I; a Serbian, frustrated with Austro-Hungarian control, assassinated the heir to the imperial throne.

North of the Balkans, Poles were also experiencing nationalist stirrings. Once a great country, Poland had been carved up between Germany, Austria-Hungary, and Russia. During the war, Poles joined together to restore their nation.

Nationalism is often cited as a cause of the war; new countries are a result of the conflict. After the war, the four empires were gone and Europe had eight new countries.

Other points encouraged mutual respect and cooperation among nations. Wilson advocated for "absolute freedom of navigation upon the seas." He called for nations to trade freely and peacefully. He asked all countries to reduce the number of weapons they had to as low a point as they needed to feel secure. These three points addressed some of the causes of the war as well as some hopes for the peace. They were idealistic, based on notions of what is right. Wilson considered firing on nonmilitary vessels immoral, even during war. He also thought that one country blocking another nation's trade was unjust. Germany's submarine warfare had been an attempt to keep countries in the Americas from doing business with Britain.

Some of the points were practical. They outlined Wilson's goals regarding specific issues created by the fighting. The armies of the Central Powers should leave the countries they invaded, land should be given back to France, Austria-Hungary should remain as a nation, and Poland should be resurrected as an independent country. These points were designed to restore or create a reasonable balance of power in Europe.

New Ideas

One revolutionary concept Wilson introduced was **self-determination**, the right of people to choose how they want to be governed. At the outbreak of the war, the major combatants—Germany, France, and Great Britain—ruled over a number of colonies in Africa, Asia, and the Middle East. Belgium, Portugal, Italy, and Spain also had colonies. With the defeat of Germany likely or at least hoped for, the fate of the German colonies was uncertain. Everyone wanted them because colonies provided raw materials, strategic advantage, and international prestige. The idealist in Wilson thought people should have a voice in their own fate. He proposed that the "interests of the populations" of the colonies "have equal weight" with the interests of the countries that ruled them. He extended the idea of self-determination to the people of various ethnic groups in Eastern Europe.

The last of the Fourteen Points was equally revolutionary. To ensure that his program was carried out, Wilson wanted countries to join together in a "general association of nations." This international association, or League of Nations, would work out the details of making and maintaining a fair peace. It would settle any future disputes that might arise between countries.

The essence of the League as Wilson envisioned it was the guarantee of **collective security**. That is, if any member nation experienced a threat to its borders or its independence, all member nations would do whatever was needed to remove that threat. Collective security meant everyone protected everyone else. Wilson believed the open commitment of all members to the safety of all the others would eliminate the need for secret alliances between individual nations.

All fourteen of Wilson's war aims were based on "the principle of justice to all peoples and nationalities, and their

LAWRENCE OF ARABIA

T. E. Lawrence (1888–1935), famous for his daring exploits in World War I, was also involved in trying to shape the peace for his beloved Arabia. The Englishman's first exposure to the Middle East was at age twenty-two on a study trip to what is now Syria. He completed his schooling in 1910 and returned to Arabia as an archaeologist. When war erupted, his knowledge of the Arabic language and culture made him valuable to the British army.

Arabia was part of the Ottoman Empire. When the empire allied itself with the Central Powers, its leaders declared a holy war against France, Britain, and Russia. The British navy depended on the oil it received from Persia, part of the empire, so England sent forces to Arabia to protect that oil supply. Lawrence's first assignment was as an interpreter, interviewing prisoners.

One strategy of the British was to use the Arabs in the empire in Britain's fight against the Ottomans, also called Turks. A desire for independence was brewing among some Arabs, and Britain stoked that desire into a rebellion. Supplying guns and money and promising Arab independence, Britain prodded the emir, or chief, of the Hejaz region to organize an Arab uprising. To succeed, the Arab revolt would need British advisors. T. E. Lawrence was among them.

Lawrence did more than show the Arabs how to use the British equipment; he joined their forces. Wearing Arab dress and riding a camel, Lawrence led Arab soldiers on guerilla raids against the Ottomans. Among his many sensational exploits were the capture of the important port of Aqaba and the destruction of seventy-nine bridges along the Hejaz Railway. He was the subject of the 1963 movie *Lawrence of Arabia*, which won seven Academy Awards.

But his dream for the Arabia he loved eluded him. A secret agreement between France and Britain erased the promise England had made of Arab independence. Lawrence went to the Paris Peace Conference with the Arab delegation to plead for an Arab state, but his pleas were denied. Lawrence of Arabia won the war but lost the peace.

right to live on equal terms of liberty and safety with one another, whether they be strong or weak." Wilson believed that if the Allies adopted his ideals, including the League that would put the ideals into practice, the world would be at peace. The conflict still raging in Europe would truly be the "final war for human liberty"—the war to end all wars.

Germany's Strategy for Peace

When Woodrow Wilson presented his Fourteen Points at the beginning of 1918, Germany's war aim was still mastery of much of Europe. Russia had just signed an armistice with the Central Powers that would give them 1 million square miles (2.6 million square kilometers) of land along with its stores of coal, oil, and iron. With Russia out of the war, Germany could shift its forces from the Eastern to the Western Front, against France. The leaders in Berlin, Germany's capital, were optimistic about the war's outcome.

However, while the political leaders believed Germany could not lose, the German generals knew their prospects for victory were fading. They were winning battles, but their casualties were heavy. They were running low not only on men but also on food, clothing, and supplies. The British blockade of their ports, intended to starve them into surrender, was working. By 1918, nearly all of Germany's cupboards were bare. Without trade with other countries, her farms could not adequately feed her people or her soldiers. The coal and iron in her soil were not adequate for weapons production.

The growing unrest at home was spreading to the army and sapping the morale of the men. Still, they fought on.

But their goal changed. The purpose of the battles for Germany in the last year of the war became to remain strong enough, capture enough territory, and inflict enough damage on the enemy to have something with which to bargain when defeat finally came. Germany expected the surrender to be conditional, the peace to be negotiated. The German army had conquered much of Belgium and large swaths of France; these could be bargaining chips in the peace-making game.

So in March, German General Erich Ludendorff launched the Spring Offensive, a series of attacks on the Western Front. He needed to grab as much ground as he could before the Americans arrived in large numbers. He wanted to negotiate surrender from a position of strength. And for a time, it appeared he might be able to pull it off. But US soldiers had begun pouring into France, two hundred thousand to three hundred thousand a month. The Second Battle of the Marne, begun July 15, turned the tide, putting the Allies on top. On September 29, Ludendorff asked the head of the Supreme Army Command, Paul von Hindenburg, to ask for a cease-fire.

The Visions Meet

The very suggestion of a truce ignited political panic in Berlin. On one side was Germany's chancellor, the primary government official, appointed by the **kaiser.** He believed

Germany could and should fight to the finish. On the other side were the military leaders, Hindenburg and Ludendorff, who basically ran the government. They knew the situation in the field was hopeless and costing lives every day. The chancellor, with little support from a war-weary government, resigned. In his place, Kaiser Wilhelm II appointed his cousin, Prince Maximilian von Baden. The new chancellor also wanted to continue the war for at least a bit, hoping a few more victories would put him in a better negotiating position. Hindenburg and Ludendorff doubted their men could win any more battles. Von Baden conceded and on October 4 composed a telegram.

The overture for an end to hostilities was not made to the battlefield generals. It was not addressed to leaders in France or England. The telegram was sent to US president Woodrow Wilson. Von Baden proposed discussing an armistice using Wilson's Fourteen Points as negotiating items. Wilson had said he wanted "peace without victory," a settlement that would not crush and humiliate the loser. Germans wanted the same thing, and the Fourteen Points was the closest they were going to get. Von Baden asked Wilson to set up a meeting at which a truce could be negotiated with all parties.

A flurry of correspondence went back and forth between the United States and Germany and the United States and the Allies. The Allied leaders were not completely on board with all fourteen of Wilson's points. Britain, with its far-flung empire and its massive navy, did not accept the idea of unfettered freedom of the seas. Neither Britain nor

Ferdinand Foch (ground level, second from right) *and other Allies stand outside Foch's train carriage on November 11, 1918.*

France was happy that **reparations** were not included. The Allies had considered Wilson's program a series of vague principles, of idealistic talk, not actual terms to be put into practice. However, Wilson was so committed to his vision he threatened to make a separate peace with Germany. That would mean withdrawing US soldiers and leaving the exhausted Allies to fight Germany alone. Instead, the Allies voiced their reservations and accepted the principles as starting points for talks.

Before talks could begin, Wilson set a firm condition on Germany. He did not trust the kaiser or the military leadership of the defeated nation and would not make any deal with them. He demanded that the kaiser abdicate—give up his throne—and civilian leaders represent the people of Germany at the negotiating table. Germany balked at the idea, and Ludendorff was ready to forget the truce and go back to battle.

But people at home as well as soldiers in the field had lost the will to fight. Most knew the war was lost. Despite the inevitability of defeat, the bloodshed would continue until a truce was signed. The German people were ready to give up. When German sailors were ordered to launch what would have been a suicide attack on the British navy, they refused. Their revolt spread beyond the military to factory workers in the cities of Germany. Continuing the combat was not possible.

Von Baden had no good option. He either agreed to Wilson's demand or watched the Allied armies overrun his country. Eager to relieve the country's misery, he sprang into action. Without the monarch's permission, he announced that Kaiser Wilhelm II had abdicated. He declared Germany a republic and turned the chancellorship over to elected leadership. All that remained was for the new government to bargain as best it could. Hindenburg sent a delegation to meet with the French supreme commander of the Allied forces to arrange a truce.

Negotiating Peace

On November 8, the German party was escorted to a remote, very private location in the Forest of Compiègne, about 37 miles (60 km) northeast of Paris. There the group was received by French general Ferdinand Fochs and British admiral Sir Rossyln Wemyss aboard Fochs's train carriage. The Germans were prepared to discuss ending hostilities according to Wilson's Fourteen Points. However, the French and the British had their own terms, which they presented in writing.

The Allies demanded that German forces leave all occupied territory and surrender massive amounts of artillery, weapons, trucks, rail vehicles, and aircraft; most of its ships; and all of its submarines. Allied troops would occupy part of Germany west of the Rhine River and establish a neutral zone on the east side of the river. The naval blockade of German ports would continue until a peace treaty could be signed. The document listed the requirement "reparation for damages done" but did not set a figure. The amount was to be decided in the peace treaty.

The terms of the truce were not negotiated; they were dictated. None were open to discussion. The bargaining chips Germany thought it had were useless; the Allies held all the cards. It was take it or leave it, sign or keep fighting. The Germans were given seventy-two hours to respond, and during that time, the war raged on.

The delegates from Berlin were horrified. They had expected something based on the Fourteen Points, not the harsh, punishing requirements before them. Their objections and their tears went unheeded. Three days later, they signed the onerous document. If these were the terms of the armistice, what would the demands of the peace treaty be?

2

Making the Peace: The Paris Peace Conference

T en weeks after the armistice went into effect, world leaders met to make the peace permanent. From the very beginning the conference was fraught with problems. Everything about it was so big as to seem impossible. There were so many nations participating, so many issues to resolve, so many demands to consider, and so many conflicting ideas of how to get anything done. Almost nothing about the conference did not begin or end in disagreement. Even the procedural items were daunting.

To begin with, where would the meeting take place? Great Britain and the United States initially wanted the peace conference held in Switzerland, which had remained neutral during the conflict. Meeting in a neutral country made sense because, technically, the war had not ended; only a cease-fire was in place pending a treaty. But reports of revolutionaries,

Opposite: Woodrow Wilson, greeted enthusiastically throughout Europe after World War I, waves to cheering crowds as he rides with French president Raymond Poincaré.

spies, and other discontented elements in Switzerland worried the negotiators. They gave in to the wishes of the French and held the conference in Paris.

Even the decision about what language would be used was contentious. The French wanted French and the English wanted English. The French argument was not that the event was to be conducted in France, but that for centuries French had been the language of trade and diplomacy. The British countered that English was fast supplanting French as the more common tongue. In addition, they pointed out, the war would not have been won without English-speaking countries. No formal agreement was reached, so all documents were presented in both languages.

The Delegates

Then there was the matter of which countries should be included. France and Britain had signed the armistice with Germany, so of course their governments should have prominent roles. Italy needed to be involved because it was, with France and Britain, part of the Supreme War Council formed in 1917 to coordinate the fighting on the Western Front. Russia was excluded because the Russians had signed a separate peace with Germany. The United States had to be present as well. Although not a formal member of the Allied coalition in the war—the United States was termed an "Associated" power—the late infusion of US troops was largely responsible for the Allied victory. Besides, the truce had been based on Wilson's Fourteen Points. Britain thought Japan should be invited to take part. Japan had fought Germans in Asia at England's request and was becoming a military and economic force in the world. These five were the major powers at the conference.

But what of the twenty-six other nations whose soldiers and sailors had fought and died? Would they have a say in the peace terms? Should their opinions count as much as those of the larger countries? What of the new states that were forming—Poland, Czechoslovakia, and others? They had been greatly affected by the war and would be greatly impacted by whatever decisions were made in the settlement. This conference would decide not only the peace but the future of Europe and of the entire world. So did the voices of neutral states matter?

What about the defeated countries? Germany expected to be a full participant—after all, a treaty was an agreement, not a surrender. Settlements also had to be reached with Austria, Hungary, Bulgaria, and the remains of the Ottoman Empire.

The major powers took it upon themselves to decide who to invite and how much influence the various countries would have. To begin with, Germany and its allies would be excluded for at least a few weeks, until the delegates came up with their peace terms. Russia was completely out for a number of reasons. Although it had fought on the Allied side, Russia had left the war early and refused to pay its debts. Besides, the major powers did not trust Russia's new government. The final count included diplomats from thirty-two countries.

The chief representative of each of the five major powers, together with each one's foreign minister, would make up the Supreme Council, also called the Council of Ten. The other delegates would be put on the fifty-eight committees established to do the detail work of the conference. The Supreme Council would figure out solutions to important questions and present its proposals at plenary sessions, where all the delegates gathered. Everyone could vote, but the vote was simply to **ratify**, or approve, what the Supreme Council decided.

Not long into the conference, the Japanese delegates found that much of the discussions did not interest them. The chief representatives of the five major powers decided they could get more done without their foreign ministers. Within two months, the Council of Ten had reduced itself to what became known as the Big Four. Even though more than seventy delegates participated, the Paris Peace Conference was basically the work of four men: Georges Clemenceau of France, David Lloyd George of Great Britain, Woodrow Wilson of the United States, and Vittorio Orlando of Italy.

The Big Four

The backgrounds, personalities, and goals of the Big Four shaped the conference proceedings and outcomes. Representing France was its prime minister, Georges Clemenceau. Clemenceau had reason to feel vengeful toward Germany. At age seventy-eight, he had personally witnessed

The Big Four (left to right): *Prime Ministers Vittorio Orlando of Italy, David Lloyd George of Britain, Georges Clemenceau of France, and US president Woodrow Wilson.*

Germany devastate his country twice. He was a young man when Germany stripped France of some of its provinces and much of its pride in 1870 and an old man when he rallied his people against German invasion in 1918. He was not embarrassed to state publicly that he hated Germany. Nicknamed "the Tiger" for his aggressiveness in political debate, he was fierce in arguing his positions at the conference. A logical and practical man, Clemenceau did not completely trust Lloyd George, and he thought Wilson far too idealistic.

Wilson certainly was idealistic. Clemenceau was right in complaining that he did not understand the history and intricacies of European relationships. The American president had assumed his fourteen principles, although somewhat vague, could be used to fix problems that were actually centuries old. Wilson had not given thought to exactly how his principles could be applied in the very real world of broken and bitter countries. The other members of the council saw Wilson as stubborn, unwilling to give up some of his ideals to accept their proposals.

Lloyd George, prime minister of England, was something of a moderator between the practical Tiger and the sometimes naïve American. He was a realistic pragmatist. He already had most of what he and Britain wanted before the conference began. England had what used to be German colonies, and the German navy was no longer a challenge to the British fleet. No battle had been fought in his country, so his war costs were small compared with those of France. Lloyd George could afford to be flexible. His cheerful, friendly disposition made him the perfect buffer between Clemenceau, who he likened to the forceful emperor Napoleon, and Wilson, who he thought fancied himself the savior of the world.

The last of the Big Four was Vittorio Orlando. The prime minister of Italy was at a disadvantage in the discussions since he could not speak English, whereas the other three could. In addition, he was not particularly popular with the Allies. Italy had begun the war as an ally of Germany and Austria-Hungary. It stayed neutral until the Allies lured it into their camp. In a secret treaty—the kind Wilson condemned in the first of his Fourteen Points—they offered Italy territory if it would help them win it. France and Britain welcomed Italy's soldiers, but they resented what they saw as its small, late, less-than-enthusiastic contribution to the war effort. For its part, Italy was interested only in getting the land it was promised. It was not concerned with what would happen to Germany. Thus, Orlando was a minor player at the conference. For all practical purposes, the Big Four was really the Big Three.

The Conference Begins

The Paris Peace Conference opened January 18, 1919. Georges Clemenceau made certain of the date. It was one celebrated in Germany. Nearly fifty years earlier, the German state of Prussia had united a number of smaller German states, going to war with France in the process. Prussia captured the French emperor and his entire army. On January 18, 1871, the victorious princes proclaimed Germany an empire. They made their proclamation not in Germany but in France, at the Palace of Versailles in Paris. Their purpose was to humiliate France. Clemenceau's deliberate choice of the opening date was meant to humiliate Germany.

German officials knew what was happening in Paris, but they were not there. The Big Four had decided to sort out their own ideas before inviting Germany to the talks. They thought of the gathering as a preconference, getting ready for the actual treaty negotiations. Wilson expected to be home in a matter of weeks. But the issues were many and difficult. The conference lasted a full year.

At the Trianon Palace Hotel in Paris, the German delegation is presented with the peace treaty on June 18, 1919. Ten days later, they signed the treaty in the Hall of Mirrors.

It was a year of hard work. The fifty-two committees that did much of the detail work held a total of 1,646 sessions. They produced reams of research, reports, analyses, and opinions. The Big Four met every day, often twice a day, for hours at a time. Their primary task was crafting a peace treaty with Germany that would satisfy all parties. Wilson, as well as the leaders of Germany, expected the treaty to incorporate his Fourteen Points. Clemenceau and Lloyd George were not sure those principles could be made to fit with the realities of European politics.

The result of the conference was the Treaty of Versailles. Among other things, it set Germany's new borders, defined its military limitations, and spelled out its financial obligations.

Borders of the New Germany

It took the delegates three months to come up with the peace treaty. Debate among the Big Four was often heated. Clemenceau, knowing that the Germans would always outnumber the French, genuinely feared that Germany would eventually attack France again. He felt he had to make Germany as small as he could, take away as much of its land as possible. He had to eliminate its military and crush its economy. He proposed cutting Germany up into a number of states, each too small to do any serious harm to France.

Neither Lloyd George nor Wilson would agree to the utter destruction of Germany, as Clemenceau's proposals would certainly accomplish. Lloyd George succeeded in tempering some of Clemenceau's demands. He promised Britain and the United States would come to France's aid in the event of a threat from any country. Still, the document that emerged, complete with 440 articles, was exceptionally harsh.

The treaty reduced Germany's size dramatically. German lands were given to Belgium, Denmark, Poland, Czechoslovakia, and Lithuania. The territory of Alsace-Lorraine, which Germany had taken from France in 1871,

POLAND: A STUDY IN NATIONALISM

The nationalistic fervor that pervaded the Paris Peace Conference was epitomized in the story of Poland. The history of Poland is a saga of nationalistic resilience in the face of external domination. Over several centuries, Poles alternated between periods of freedom and prosperity and oppression from other countries. They fought off invasions and control by the Mongols, the Teutonic Knights, Swedes, Russians, and Turks. Every time they were overtaken, they rose in defiance. They maintained the Kingdom of Poland, even when foreigners put their own kings on Poland's throne.

In the eighteenth century, their aggressive neighbors proved too strong for them. In the last quarter of that century, Poland was divided three times among Prussia, Austria, and Russia. Each time the more powerful nations took a little more of the country for themselves until in 1795 there was nothing left; Poland ceased to exist. Rather than remain among their oppressors, many Poles fled to Italy and France.

The death of their country did not kill the Poles' spirits. Pride in their Polish identity, which had sustained them through centuries of challenges, remained strong. The loss of their land gave fresh fuel to Polish nationalism. The song that would become their national anthem begins, "Poland is not yet lost as long as we live. We will fight for all that our enemies have taken from us." The words were penned in 1795, just after other countries thought they had buried any hope of a nation of Poland.

True to their song, the Poles, without a country, fought for what their enemies had taken from them. Thousands formed military units called the Polish Legions and joined Napoleon against Russia and Austria. After Napoleon's defeat, the victors resurrected a small Kingdom of Poland, but it was not an independent state; it was ruled and eventually **annexed** by Russia. When resistance movements and rebellions failed to gain real independence for their nation, Poles focused their undying pride in being Polish on strengthening their national identity. They built strong cultural organizations, educational efforts, and political parties.

In World War I, Poles fought on both sides because some lived in Germany, some in Austria, and some in Russia. However, their loyalty was not to their country, but to their Polish nationality. The defeat of all three countries (Russia lost to the Central Powers before the Central Powers lost to the Allies) raised the possibility that an independent Poland could rise from their ashes. Wilson's thirteenth point encouraged that hope: "An independent Polish state should be erected which should include the territories inhabited by indisputably Polish populations." Whether that would happen was up to the delegates at the Paris Peace Conference.

was returned. Not counting its colonies, all of which were taken away, Germany lost 13 percent of its land and almost seven million of its population.

Clemenceau wanted to take the Saar region as well. This was a small area on the German-French border. It was the heart of Germany's industrial strength, rich in coal and home to many factories. Lloyd George, however, was not willing to deprive Germany of its ability to recover economically. Clemenceau had to accept a compromise. France could have the coal mines, but an international body, the League of Nations, would control the Saar for fifteen years. After that, the people of the region would vote on whether to stay under the rule of the League or be part of Germany or France.

The territory along the Rhine River, on the border with France, was of great concern to Clemenceau. France had always claimed that its land should extend to the Rhine, but Germany held territory on both sides of the river. Now the prime minister wanted the western portion of the Rhineland. At the very least, he insisted on some protection from the possibility of invasion. The solution was the establishment of a **demilitarized zone**.

It was not completely demilitarized, which means free of any soldiers. It was free of all German military. One of the terms of the armistice was that Germany had to remove all its forces and fortifications in the Rhineland. The west bank of the river—the area France wanted for itself—would be "administered by the local troops of **occupation**," the armies of the Allies and the United States. The occupation would extend to part of the east bank also. The treaty extended the distance on the east bank to 31 miles (50 km). Clemenceau wanted the occupation to be permanent, but Lloyd George and Wilson overruled him. The Frenchman had to settle for a term of fifteen years.

French soldiers patrolling the demilitarized Rhineland view the town of Koblenz, where the Mosel and Rhine Rivers come together, in 1929.

Military Restrictions

Demilitarization of a sensitive plot of ground, at least for a short time, made sense to the negotiators. But how much military might should be taken away from Germany? If he could have had his way, Clemenceau would have taken it all. However, the other leaders were concerned about a growing threat east of Germany. Russia was a huge country with huge ambitions. Talk in Russia about worldwide revolution worried many in Europe. Lloyd George felt that Germany, with its strong military knowledge and ability, was Europe's best bet for keeping Russia in check.

Point number four of Wilson's Fourteen Points called for the armaments of all countries to "be reduced to the lowest point consistent with domestic safety." Where was that point for Germany in 1919? The Big Four decided it was quite low. The treaty allowed Germany an army of no more than one hundred thousand men, a far cry from the thirteen million who had served in the war. There could be no draft; any army Germany could muster would have to be made up of volunteers. The country could have only three schools for training military officers. Those officers and men could have no tanks and no heavy artillery. The treaty included tables detailing exactly how the tiny army was to be organized and how many of what types of weapons and ammunition it could have.

Restrictions on Germany's sea and air power were even more severe. The current navy had to be forfeited to Great Britain, a term that greatly pleased Lloyd George. In the future, the German navy was limited to thirty-six vessels: six battleships, six light cruisers, twelve destroyers, and twelve torpedo boats. The sizes of these ships were specified in the treaty. Absolutely no submarines were permitted. The officer corps could not exceed fifteen hundred men.

Airplanes had made their military debut in World War I, and Germany was at the forefront of the innovation. Fighter pilots, such as Manfred von Richthofen, the famous Red Baron, had caused considerable damage to Allied forces. Generals were just beginning to see the potential of planes in warfare, and the Big Four wanted to make sure their former enemy did not have access to this promising weapon. Article 198 of the treaty stated, "The armed forces of Germany must not include any military or naval air forces."

Wilson had hoped limiting Germany's ability to wage war would encourage all countries to reduce their armaments. However, nothing in the treaty required any nation except Germany to give up its arms. The terms were "consistent with [the] domestic safety" of France, Britain, and other countries, but Germans saw them as a threat to its domestic safety.

Reparations

Guaranteeing the safety of France was only one of Clemenceau's goals. Money was another. As with the other Allies, France had spent a great deal in the war and would need to spend more restoring all that had been damaged. Clemenceau thought it only just that Germany foot the bill for all of it. No battle had been fought on German soil, whereas huge swaths of France and Belgium had been laid to waste.

It was not unusual for the victor in war to require some financial compensation from the loser. One form of compensation is **indemnity**, which is payment of war costs. It covers expenses associated with soldiers, armaments, and fortifications. Another form of compensation is reparations, so called because they are intended to repair some of the harm caused by the war. Typically, reparations make up for losses to the civilian populations. Which would it be: indemnity or reparations?

The Big Three had very different views on the matter, and they disagreed fiercely. Clemenceau pushed for heavy reparations. He needed to rebuild the roads, bridges, factories, and cities the German troops had destroyed. He knew that whatever money they could squeeze out of Germany would be limited. If the payments were reparations, France and Belgium, the two countries most heavily damaged, would get the lion's share.

Lloyd George argued for an indemnity. Britain could claim no civilian losses; the fighting had harmed neither the English countryside nor ordinary British citizens. Britain's immense war cost was in military men and materials, which an indemnity would cover. Lloyd George did not want to cripple Germany financially as Clemenceau did, but if money was going to be paid out, he wanted some of it for Britain.

Wilson insisted there be no indemnity. The armistice had said "reparation," he reminded his fellow delegates, so reparation it would have to be. Germany could be made to pay only for civilian damages. Lloyd George still managed to have

REPARATIONS PAYMENTS

All five World War I peace treaties demanded reparations and left the amount to be determined by the Reparation Committee. Some could be paid in materials and some was required in cash. The countries had great difficulty paying, and adjustments had to be made to the demands and the schedules. The amount each nation was charged and the amounts they paid are in the chart below.

Country	Treaty	Amount Assessed	Payments Made
Germany	Versailles	132 billion gold marks ($33 billion)	23 billion gold marks ($5.75 billion) by 1931, at least $1 billion more after 1980.
Austria	Saint-Germain-en-Laye	Amount left to Reparation Commission	215,000 square miles (556,847 sq km) in land loss considered sufficient
Hungary	Trianon	10 million gold crowns per year for twenty years	Suspended due to inability to pay
Bulgaria	Neuilly-sur-Seine	2.25 billion gold francs ($445 million)	$214 million
Ottoman Empire (Turkey)	Sèvres	All claims for reparations waived	None

some of the payout allotted to Britain. He convinced Wilson to include pensions for wounded soldiers and allowances for war widows under reparations, even though these items were clearly war costs.

The War Guilt Clause

The Allies felt they needed to include in the treaty the justification for their financial demands. That justification, the first paragraph in the Reparations section of the document, was Article 231, infamously known as the War Guilt Clause:

"

The Allied and Associated Governments affirm and Germany accepts the responsibility of Germany and her allies for causing all the loss and damage to which the Allied and Associated Governments and their nationals have been subjected as a consequence of the war imposed upon them by the aggression of Germany and her allies.

"

The article basically says, "Germany and her allies caused the war and all harm associated with it." Logically, then, Germany should pay for all the damage. In Article 233, the Allies admitted that "the resources of Germany are not adequate ... to make complete reparation for all such loss and damage." In other words, Germany did not have enough money to pay the total amount it owed the Allies—estimated at almost $126 billion. So the treaty limited reparations to "compensation for all damage done to the civilian population of the Allied and Associated Powers and to their property."

Exactly how much was that? Not surprisingly, no one could agree. Wilson wanted to base the reparation on what the German economy could be expected to produce. He suggested $28.5 billion. Clemenceau and Lloyd George considered that number ridiculously small. Unable to settle on a figure after months of wrangling, and pressed to get on with other matters, the Big Four postponed the decision. They created a reparation commission and gave it two years to come up with an amount and a payment schedule.

In the meantime, the treaty stated, Germany must pay an initial reparation of 20 billion gold marks ($4.76 billion). These funds were to be used to pay the Allies for the costs of occupying German land.

The League of Nations

Reparations, military restrictions, and national borders were pressing matters for Europe's leaders, but for Woodrow Wilson, there was a much more important topic for the delegates in Paris. Wilson wanted the first order of business at the conference to be a discussion of "a general association of nations" that could guarantee the safety and security of "great and small states alike." It was the last of his Fourteen Points. Wilson believed that establishment of a league of peace-loving nations committed to international rather than national interests would be able to keep the peace the treaty would produce. Convincing others of that belief became his mission.

The others of the Big Four gave in to the American president. One week after the conference opened they formed a commission on the League of Nations with Wilson as its head. As with so many topics facing the delegates at the conference, disagreements surfaced. Some did not like the idea of reducing their countries' arms. The French delegates thought the League should have an army, but the British worried that France would dominate such a force. Wilson also rejected the idea of an international military. Japan suggested including a statement affirming racial equality, but that idea was dismissed. The commission worked through the differences and within two weeks produced a draft of the Covenant of the League of Nations.

Wilson proudly presented the draft to the plenary session. The delegates then discussed its provisions with their respective leaders. After a few minor adjustments, the Covenant of the League of Nations became the first section of the Treaty of Versailles.

The covenant was basically the constitution of the new organization. It detailed the structure and functioning of the League. It spelled out who could be part of it, what types of issues it would deal with, and how it would deal with them. The first members would be all the countries that signed the treaty except Germany. After that, membership was open to any nation that agreed to the stipulations of the covenant and was approved by two-thirds of the sitting members.

The organization was fairly simple, consisting of three bodies: an assembly, a council, and a secretariat. In the General Assembly, made up of representatives of all members, people could bring up and discuss any matter "affecting the peace of the world." The actual decisions were made by the Council, which consisted of representatives of what were termed the Principle Allied (France, Britain, Italy, and Japan) and Associated (United States) Powers as permanent members and representatives of four other countries as rotating members. The Secretariat was an administrative body, the staff that took care of the details that kept the organization functioning.

The League was the first attempt to tackle large issues through international consensus rather than through alliances between countries. Its main responsibility was to prevent disputes between countries and, if it couldn't prevent problems, to resolve them peacefully. Wilson got two of his Fourteen Points into the covenant: international arms reduction and an end to secret agreements. He lobbied for freedom of the seas, but the British blocked him. The covenant envisioned not only maintaining peace but also promoting justice and well-being. It established a Permanent Court of International Justice and provided for an International Labor Organization, a Health Organization, and a number of commissions to find solutions to international concerns such as refugees, drug trafficking, and child welfare.

In this 1919 cartoon, US president Woodrow Wilson is depicted as having difficulty applying his Fourteen Points to the competing interests of European nations.

For Woodrow Wilson, the League of Nations was the best hope for the future of the world. There were flaws in the treaty, but the League could fix them. There would be disagreements about how to implement the terms of the treaty, but the League could get people to work out their differences. There was unfinished business in the treaty, but the League could wrap up the loose ends. Wilson was firmly convinced the League of Nations would make wars things of the past.

By the end of April, the Treaty of Versailles was finished. It contained the Covenant of the League of Nations and the terms the Allies would present to Germany. More work remained to be done, such as writing treaties for Austria, Hungary, Bulgaria, and the Ottoman Empire and deciding what was to be done with Germany's colonies. These items would take considerable time and some could be left to the League. What could not wait was formally ending the war. In May 1919, the immediate matter before the delegates was getting Germany to sign the treaty.

Instruments
of Peace

Germany eagerly awaited its invitation to the Paris Peace Conference. The original plan was for the Allies to agree on one list of peace terms and then meet with Germany. The two sides would present their proposals, discuss where they differed, compromise where they could, and arrive at final terms. This was the way treaties were made, through respectful negotiation.

The Germans were optimistic they could barter a decent settlement. The country was now a republic, not really the same nation that had waged the disastrous war. It would not be the generals or the kaiser negotiating, but a brand-new, democratically elected government. Although the harshness of the armistice had surprised them, they believed they could appeal to Wilson's Fourteen Points. So the German Foreign

Opposite: German citizens protest in front of the Reichstag, Germany's parliament, on May 15, 1919, urging their leaders not to sign the Treaty of Versailles.

Ministry worked diligently to develop its proposal, prepare its arguments, and gather materials to support its case.

Enemies Meet

The war had been over nearly six months before the German delegates were called to the conference. Their reception there did not bode well for the negotiations. First, the French train that brought them to Paris slowed deliberately as it crept through northeastern France. The delegates could not avoid the panoramic views of the French countryside devastated by their soldiers. When they finally reached their destination, they were not taken to the luxury hotels that housed other delegations. Their hotel was surrounded by barbed wire and guarded by armed men.

On May 7, 1919, the German delegates were ushered into the reception salon of the Trianon Palace Hotel. Clemenceau presented them with the document over which the Allies had labored so long. He gave them two weeks to digest its 440 articles. If they had any comments, they could submit them in writing. That was to be the extent of the negotiations.

The Germans were stunned. Neither the way they were treated nor the treaty itself were anything close to what they had expected. They were especially offended by Article 231, the clause that said Germany bore full responsibility for all the damages the war had wrought. The Allies had not realized the item would arouse such bitterness; they had inserted it only to have a legal basis for demanding reparations. But to the Germans, it was false, demeaning, and dishonorable.

With great restraint, the leader of the German delegation, Count von Brockdorff-Rantzau, penned a calm, reasoned response. After all, he had come to negotiate. He reminded the Allies they had understood the peace would be based on Wilson's Fourteen Points. Instead, he had been handed terms that were impossible. They were, he wrote, "more than the German people can bear."

Von Brockdorff-Rantzau listed some of the impossible terms and offered counter-proposals. He pointed out that he had not been given sufficient time to make more complete suggestions for compromise. Negotiating through notes was difficult and ineffective; the count requested face-to-face talks.

On behalf of the Allies, Clemenceau responded with a long list of complaints against Germany, stretching from before the war. Making clear that his letter was the final Allied word, he gave the count two choices: "The treaty in its present form must be accepted or rejected." As he wrote, General Fochs, the Allies' supreme military commander, was standing by with his army, ready to resume the fighting if the treaty was rejected.

Signing the Treaty

The delegation returned to Germany with the appalling news. The reaction of the people, the military, and the government was disbelief and rage. Angry citizens protested loudly. A German admiral, waiting in Scotland with the ships that had been surrendered at the armistice, scuttled, or purposely sank, the entire fleet to keep them from the Allies.

The chancellor resigned rather than be forced to sign the degrading document. The president considered returning to battle, but his generals told him they would lose. Because of the disarray in the government, Germany asked for a forty-eight-hour delay. The Allies refused. With only hours to spare before the final deadline, the president wired his decision to Paris. Germany would sign.

On June 28, leaders and diplomats from all over the world gathered at Versailles. Clemenceau had orchestrated a very dramatic event, dripping with pain and humiliation for the German delegation. The setting was the Palace of Versailles, home to Louis XIV in the 1600s, when France

An official directs Georges Clemenceau (center, at desk) *where to sign the Treaty of Versailles.*

was the undisputed leader of Europe. The room was the Hall of Mirrors, lavishly adorned with magnificent chandeliers, ornate windows, and 578 sparkling mirrors. Paintings on the ceilings recorded the exploits and victories of the French king. Clemenceau relished bringing the vanquished Germans into this extravagant room. It told them France was the winner.

The French prime minister had another reason for choosing the Hall of Mirrors. In 1871, Germans—then Prussians—and French had met in this very place. It was the end of the Franco-Prussian War and France had lost. The Prussians had come to France, to the Palace of Versailles, to proclaim the beginning of the German Empire … and to gloat. Clemenceau had seen that day, and he remembered it with bitterness. Now it was his turn to gloat.

To stage his revenge, Clemenceau sat in the exact spot where the Prussians had stood almost fifty years earlier. He placed the writing desk of Louis XIV in the center of the room. On the front row, he seated soldiers who had been horribly wounded in the war. The Germans would have to walk past them. He opened several of the seventeen windows so the Germans could hear the cannons and cheers celebrating the signing that marked their defeat. He ordered that the fountains of Versailles that had been shut down since the beginning of the war be turned on as soon as the Germans signed the treaty.

Just after 3 p.m., the German delegates were ushered into the Hall of Mirrors, already packed with diplomats, military officers, and reporters. Clemenceau opened the

THE GERMAN SIGNERS

The period from the last days of the fighting to the signing of the peace treaty was total chaos in the government of Germany. In that brief span of time, workers staged more than five hundred strikes, sailors mutinied, the kaiser abdicated, chancellors resigned, and a republic was declared. As Communists, centrists, and Social Democrats vied for control, revolts and assassinations rocked the country. This was the political situation when Count von Brockdorff-Rantzau brought the draft of the Treaty of Versailles to his country's leaders.

Despite intense anger and disbelief, the treaty had to be signed. Who would perform the dreaded but necessary task? No German wanted his name on the document that immortalized Germany's utter defeat and humiliating admission of guilt for World War I. Several people resigned their positions rather than have their names forever connected with the treaty of shame. The chore fell to two men: Hermann Müller and Johannes Bell.

Müller was a leader of the Social Democratic Party, a party of the working class. He had climbed his way up in the party, championing causes of the common man. Bell had a more privileged upbringing. He was a jurist—a lawyer and legal scholar. Politically, Bell was a member of the German Centre Party, a group that supported the kaiser. When Germany was forced to form a democratic government, both Müller and Bell were elected to the National Assembly, the republic's parliament.

The Allies had insisted that the two people who signed the peace treaty on behalf of Germany have positions of standing in the German government. The turmoil in the government made that difficult. Between the time von Brockdorff-Rantzau presented the treaty to the National Assembly and the deadline for signing, the chancellor had resigned and no one knew for certain who could represent the government in Versailles. A new chancellor, a Social Democrat, assumed leadership in June 1919 and hastily appointed Müller foreign minister. He kept Bell on as colonial minister.

Müller was in his position only seven days when he signed the treaty. Bell was colonial minister, but the minute he signed the treaty Germany no longer had any colonies for him to administer. Both men resigned from politics as Adolf Hitler rose to power.

proceedings with only a few sentences and then directed the Germans to the signing desk. Following the Germans, representatives of thirty-one other nations stepped forward to sign. The ceremony was over in less than an hour. Probably by coincidence, the event that ended the war occurred on the fifth anniversary of the shooting of the Austrian archduke, the incident that began the conflict.

Presenting the Treaty to America

American president Woodrow Wilson signed the treaty, but his signature did not commit the United States to its terms. The US Constitution requires two-thirds of the Senate to ratify treaties before they can become law. The Senate had already rejected part of the treaty, the part that was most important to Wilson. Immediately after drawing up the Covenant of the League of Nations, Wilson had left the peace conference for a short trip to Washington, DC, to present his achievement to Congress. But Congress had not been impressed. Now that the treaty, which included the League of Nations, had been signed by twenty-eight nations, Wilson's new mission was to win Senate ratification.

Probably the main reason the Senate did not approve the covenant was political. Wilson was a Democrat. He had been elected to a second term in 1916 by a very slim margin, touting the fact that he had kept America out of the war in Europe. But after the election he talked Congress into entering that war. Many people throughout the country were

In his 1915 State of the Union address, Wilson spoke to a Congress wary of war; in his 1919 speeches, he addressed a Congress wary of the peace.

isolationist. They did not want America involved in Europe's problems. Unhappy with Wilson, they voted Republican in the midterm elections of 1918. That made Republicans the majority in both houses of Congress.

The most influential Republican in the Senate was the majority leader, Henry Cabot Lodge. He was also chairman of the Senate Foreign Relations Committee, so he led all discussion in the Senate on matters involving foreign countries. Lodge was very powerful and very outspoken— and he detested Wilson. The two were on opposite ends of the political spectrum; Lodge was conservative and Wilson was liberal. Lodge was practical and Wilson was idealistic. They disagreed strongly on many issues.

Unlike many of his Democratic Senate colleagues, however, Lodge was not an isolationist. He chaired the Foreign Relations Committee because he believed America should be involved in world affairs. He saw the war as a struggle between right and wrong and felt America should be a force for right. Lodge was disturbed with Wilson's early insistence on US neutrality. When the United States finally declared war on Germany, Lodge criticized what he saw as Wilson's weak leadership.

Wilson's leadership style may have been another reason for his failure to get Senate approval of the Covenant of the League of Nations. When he announced that he planned to participate in the peace conference, he did not consult a single Republican. He took a large delegation of diplomats, military officers, and politicians, but he included only one Republican, one who often shared his Democratic views. He knew that when the conference produced a treaty he would have to sell the treaty to the Senate, yet he did not invite one senator to accompany him to Paris. Furthermore, at the peace conference he barely consulted with any of the US delegates. He preferred to act alone.

Debate Over Ratification

When Wilson returned to the United States with the treaty in hand, he met strong resistance in Congress. A few senators were unhappy with the harshness of the terms for Germany. Most of the objections, however, had to do with the League of Nations. Some Congressmen were isolationists; they rejected the idea of US involvement with any multinational group.

Henry Cabot Lodge, who led the opposition to the treaty, was actually in favor of an international organization to enforce peace. He was happy with America having a lead role in such a world body. But he didn't like Wilson's league. His main objection was Article X, which stated:

> *The Members of the League undertake to respect and preserve as against external aggression the territorial integrity and existing political independence of all Members of the League. In case of any such aggression or in case of any threat or danger of such aggression the Council shall advise upon the means by which this obligation shall be fulfilled.*

Article X required that the countries that joined the League would respect the borders of all other member countries. Senators agreed with that provision. But the article also said the members would "undertake" to "preserve" those borders if anyone attacked or even threatened to attack them. In other words, the United States would have to come to the aid of Belgium, Greece, Japan, or any other League nation if it were in danger. Even more troubling to many Senators, the Council of the League would decide exactly what aid the United States should supply or how America should react to aggression. The League could require America to cut diplomatic relations with another country, refuse to trade or do business with some nation, or send the US military into battle almost anywhere in the world.

Lodge did not want any country or association of countries to make decisions for the United States, even if the United States had a representative in the association. He was particularly adamant that no international body should commit American soldiers to war. In the US Constitution, only Congress can declare war. Agreeing to the Covenant of the League of Nations would give the League Council the power that belonged to Congress alone.

Lodge was not the only senator opposed to the treaty and its League of Nations. The ninety-six senators were split among three distinct factions. One faction consisted of the supporters. The supporters—nearly all Democrats—were loyal to Wilson. They accepted the treaty just as the president presented it to them, including the League. Second were the reservationists. They approved of parts of the treaty but had reservations, or objections, about other parts. They wanted to amend the treaty, to add provisions that would change the sections they didn't like.

The third faction was called the **Irreconcilables**. That was the name given to a group of about fifteen senators, both Republican and Democrat, who refused to accept the Treaty of Versailles in any form whatsoever. Most were isolationists. They were especially wary of involvements outside the Western hemisphere. A few were so against foreign intervention they had voted against America's entry into World War I.

Lodge appeared to be in the reservationist group. He wanted an association of peace-loving nations—just not Wilson's association. He had two reasons for opposing the treaty. One: he had real objections to some aspects of the League, especially Article X. Two: he was against anything Wilson was for.

When the president returned from Paris with the treaty, the people received the news gladly. The war was really over and a new, peaceful world seemed possible. Public opinion was with Wilson. Lodge needed to make a case against the treaty, to win public support and Senate votes to his side. As chairman of the committee that presented the matter to the Senate, he could drag out the debate on ratification. He used several delaying tactics, such as insisting on reading the entire treaty aloud in his committee. That action alone took up two weeks.

Taking the Fight to the People

After six weeks of fruitless discussion by the Senate, Wilson was frustrated. He decided to sell the idea of the treaty—or, more specifically, the League of Nations—directly to the people. If he could gain enough public support for his dream, the citizens might persuade their senators to vote for it. Wilson did not have much time; the treaty was to go

GOING TO TALK TO THE BOSS

In this 1919 cartoon, President Wilson is depicted as a salesman, barging past the Senate and the House to present the League of Nations to the American people.

into effect January 10, 1920. If the Senate did not ratify it by that date, the United States would not be part of the League.

On September 3, 1919, President Wilson began his campaign. It was a whirlwind trip by train, covering 8,000 miles (12,875 km) in twenty-two days. Wilson gave passionate speeches, rallying many throughout the West and Midwest to his vision. He tried to convince them that isolationism was no longer good for America. Events in distant parts of the globe would eventually seep or explode beyond national borders and come to US shores. He reminded them that the last war had begun in Europe but spread to Asia, Africa, and the Americas. Ignoring other countries' problems was dangerous, he warned. A confederation of nations that promised to respect and protect one another's independence would ensure peace.

Wilson appealed to people's patriotic spirit. The League embodied America's ideals, he told them. It was based on the principle of freedom to determine one's own government. It encouraged open discussion, cooperation, righting wrongs, and helping those in need. He emphasized the League's programs for abolishing slavery, improving labor conditions, and promoting health. The League would create a world not only without war, but growing in prosperity. America must be a part, a leader, in bringing about such a world.

Wilson delivered this message thirty-eight times and would have continued, but he collapsed in Pueblo, Colorado, and was rushed back to Washington. A week later, he had a severe stroke that paralyzed much of the left side of his body. The sudden stroke ended his campaign, but he was not yet defeated. The Senate still had to vote.

The Treaty's Fate

In Wilson's absence, Lodge had come up with a new approach for defeating ratification of the treaty. He compiled the objections senators had raised to the treaty into a list of fourteen reservations. When the Foreign Relations Committee presented the treaty to the Senate, the reservations

THE FIRST WOMAN PRESIDENT

When Woodrow Wilson suffered a stroke on October 2, 1919, very few people knew how seriously ill the president was. The medical bulletins from the White House said only that Wilson needed rest. He was exhausted from his three-week speaking tour and needed time to recover. He would be conducting the country's business from his bed.

Those bulletins were issued by his wife. Edith was Wilson's second wife; they had been married almost four years when the stroke incapacitated him. Throughout their short time together, she had managed to keep his frail health a secret. Not many people were aware of the intense headaches that plagued him during his cross-country railroad tour. Even fewer knew how close to death he had come when stricken with influenza in Paris.

After his stroke, Edith stood guard over her husband. She refused to let the world see that the sixty-three-year-old president could not move his left arm. Almost no one—White House staff, cabinet ministers, Congressmen—got farther than the West Sitting Room, where Edith maintained her station. She read every paper presented to the president, carried the ones she considered important into his room, and emerged with his responses scrawled on the documents.

Edith knew quite well how the presidency functioned. From the moment she became first lady, she shared her husband's office in the White House. She screened his mail, sat in on his meetings, and shared her opinions.

She had access to classified materials. When Wilson went to the peace conference, she was by his side. So even though the president was confined to his bed after his stroke, Edith saw no reason he should resign. She could handle his responsibilities for him.

As Wilson's physical absence from affairs of state began to trouble cabinet officials and Congressmen, they urged Vice President Thomas Marshall to declare himself acting president. Marshall adamantly refused. He took over some presidential duties, such as presiding over cabinet meetings, but he would not take Wilson's place without a formal resignation or a congressional resolution. So for the last year and a half of his term, Edith Wilson was, for all intents and purposes, president of the United States. One senator called that brief period the "petticoat government."

had been added. The vote was not on the treaty Wilson had signed at Versailles but on the treaty with the reservations.

The reservations stated the parts of the treaty with which the United States disagreed. Where the United States disagreed, it could not follow what the treaty said should be done. The reservations explained what the US government would do instead if it signed the treaty. Ratifying a treaty with reservations basically said, "We agree to most of the treaty and promise to comply, but we will not do certain specific things written in the document."

Some of Lodge's reservations were minor, but one struck at the most important part of the League of Nations. The foundation of the League was the guarantee of collective security. That is, countries were secure knowing that if they were threatened, other nations would fight with and for them. Article X of the treaty gave the League the responsibility to decide when war was warranted and required all member nations to go to war if the League so ordered. The reservation rejected that requirement. It stated that the United States would not engage in any military action ordered by the League unless the US Congress approved of that action. Lodge's reservation basically said the United States did not have to comply with Article X.

Lodge knew Wilson would never consent to this reservation. To the president, the Covenant of the League of Nations was the heart of the treaty and Article X was the core of the covenant. As much as Wilson wanted the Senate to ratify the treaty, he could not accept a treaty gutted of its

Henry Cabot Lodge, seen here in 1923, served in the Massachusetts House of Representatives, the US House, and the US Senate from 1880 to 1924.

most vital element. Unable to compromise, the president urged the supporters to vote against the version of the treaty presented to them, the treaty with reservations. Since the Irreconcilables also voted against it, it fell seven votes short of the two-thirds needed for ratification. Four months later, the Senate considered the treaty again. Again, it was defeated. Wilson was awarded the 1919 Nobel Peace Prize for his creation of the League of Nations, but neither he nor the United States was ever a part of that League.

Peace at Last

The Senate's failure to ratify the Treaty of Versailles meant that the United States was, technically at least, still at war with Germany. The United States had not signed the armistice. As long as the two countries remained at war, they could not have diplomatic relations, American companies could not trade with Germany, and the United States could have no voice in how the Allies treated their former enemy. Warren Harding, who succeeded Wilson as president, asked Congress to remedy the situation. The House of Representatives and the Senate together created the Knox-Porter Resolution, which simply stated that "the state of war declared to exist between the Imperial German Government and the United States of America ... is hereby declared at an end."

When Harding signed the joint resolution on July 2, 1919, the two countries were at peace, but the terms of that peace still needed to be decided. Toward that end, representatives of the United States and Germany met in Berlin in August and actually negotiated a treaty. The document, officially titled the Treaty between the United States and Germany Restoring Friendly Relations, maintained most of the provisions in the Treaty of Versailles but without the oversight of the League of Nations.

The Treaty of Versailles dealt only with Germany. Separate treaties had to be made between the Allies and the other Central Powers. The United States had declared war only on Germany, so it was not involved in those arrangements. Between September 1919 and August 1920, four treaties brought World War I to a close. The Treaty of Saint-Germain-en-Laye and Trianon dissolved the Austro-Hungarian Empire, replacing it with the Republic of Austria, and the Treaty of Trianon settled matters with Hungary. Bulgaria made peace by the Treaty of Neuilly-sur-Seine. The Treaty of Sèvres, replaced in 1923 with the Treaty of Lausanne, dealt with Turkey and the other parts of the fractured Ottoman Empire. Peace had finally come, but many problems remained.

Keeping
the Peace?

I n calling World War I "the war to end all wars," Woodrow Wilson put his hopes in the Treaty of Versailles with its provision for a League of Nations. Wars could be averted, he believed, if the principles he strove to write into the treaty were widely accepted and steadfastly followed. Those principles were national self-determination, rejection of secret treaties, international disarmament, and the collective security provided by an association of peace-loving nations.

The sad truth, apparent twenty years after Versailles, is that neither the treaty nor the League kept war from happening. The plan was for the peace conference to draw the dividing lines for a new, peaceful world and the League of Nations to see that the lines stayed firm. But the plan was flawed from the beginning. Lines could not be drawn

Opposite: *The female figure on this monument to the Czech Legions that fought on the side of the Allies represents the city of Prague. The inscription reads, "Prague to her victorious sons."*

that would satisfy everyone, and the League could not keep countries from overstepping the assigned boundaries.

The New Map of Europe

The first step in making peace had been to settle borders. The collapse of empires left a lot of land without rulers, and the rise of nationalism created a number of parties laying claim to different parts of that land. The normal way of handling the situation had been for the winners to divide up the territory of the losers—"to the victors belong the spoils." But Wilson introduced a new element into the calculation, designed to prevent wars: national self-determination.

In his Fourteen Points, Wilson put forward the idea that people had the right to govern themselves. Furthermore, he contended, national self-government was the basis for international peace. He reasoned that states that determined their own course would be content and have no reason to attack another. In Austria-Hungary and the Ottoman Empire before the war, people of many cultures, or nationalities, were ruled by emperors of a completely different culture. Wilson proposed that these national groups, bound together by a common language, values, and history, be given independence and allowed to determine their own form of government. Wilson pushed hard to have the principle of national self-government recognized in the Treaty of Versailles' Covenant of the League of Nations.

The principle was the basis of nine new states in Europe. Four were carved out of the Austro-Hungarian Empire somewhat along national or ethnic lines. Austria went to German-speaking Austria and Hungary to ethnic Hungarians. The Czechs were given their own state, which they called Czechoslovakia. Some land from the empire became part of Serbia, and the people there created the new nation of Yugoslavia.

Another four states were carved out of German territory. Before losing to the Allies, Germany had gained land from Russia along the eastern coast of the Baltic Sea. But the people in those lands did not want to submit to either Russia or Germany. In the confusing final days of the war and amid a tumultuous revolution in Russia, the three Baltic states of Estonia, Latvia, and Lithuania, together with Finland, declared their independence. The Allies, proclaiming their right to self-determination, recognized them as **sovereign** states. That is, they were free and independent countries.

Poland

The ninth new European nation was Poland. In 1914, Poland did not exist; the Polish people had long been divided among Germany, Austria, and Russia. But during the war they united behind their dream of a resurrected Poland. There was no question—at least for Woodrow Wilson—that Poland would emerge from the war as an independent state. That was one of his Fourteen Points. By the time the armistice was signed, a Republic of Poland had been declared. However, Poles were scattered over a vast area; where were the borders of the new republic? The Allies decided that at Versailles. They drew the boundaries of Poland to include West Prussia (formerly part of Germany), part of the Ukraine (from Russia), and a section of Austria.

In addition to "an independent Polish state … inhabited by indisputably Polish populations," Wilson's Fourteen Points called for Poland to have "a free and secure access to the sea." To achieve this, the Allies gave Poland a strip of Germany that would connect it to the Baltic Sea. This land, called the Polish Corridor, had belonged to Poland before the country was divided in the eighteenth century and its population was largely Polish. But the corridor separated the German territory of East Prussia from the rest of Germany.

At the northern end of the Polish Corridor, on the Baltic Sea, was the port of Danzig. Unlike in the rest of the corridor, the people of Danzig and the area around it were predominantly German. The Allies faced a dilemma; they had made two competing promises. On the one hand, they had said they would give Poland access to the sea. On the other hand, they were committed to the principle of self-determination and Danzig was German. The solution was to award the port to neither Poland nor Germany. The Treaty of Versailles made Danzig a free city under the rule of the League of Nations. The Free City of Danzig encompassed the city and more than three hundred surrounding towns and villages, an area of 754 square miles (1,952 sq km).

Dissatisfaction with the Lines

The case of Danzig illustrates the difficulty of the Allies' approach to drawing borders. Like much of Europe, the city housed more than one national group. Which group was entitled to self-government? The treaty returned the province of Alsace-Lorraine to France, but many Germans there wanted to remain with Germany. None of the nine new countries that emerged from the peace conference contained only one cultural group, and the minorities were often unhappy with the new arrangements.

Germans were particularly unhappy. The creation of the Free City and the nine new countries was based on Wilson's principle of national self-government. However, that principle was not applied to Germans. The citizens of Austria were German in language and culture, but the treaty forbade Germany and Austria from merging. Poland and Lithuania had sizeable German communities, but they were not allowed to form their own states. The Sudetenland, an area in the Sudetes Mountains, was ethnically German, but the Allies gave it to Czechoslovakia. The treaty touted self-determination of peoples as a sacred value but denied it to Germans.

In the interwar years, the dissatisfaction grew into bitterness. Adolf Hitler used the smoldering feelings of injustice to rally Germans scattered in other countries to a nationalistic identity. When he announced the Anschluss, or annexation, of Austria in 1938, many Germans living in

Austria felt he was justified. Germans in the Sudetenland cheered when his army marched into Czechoslovakia. These actions, the immediate prelude to World War II, were seen as righting the wrongs of Versailles.

Of all the inequities in the treaty's reallocation of land, probably the most glaring for Germany was the Polish Corridor. Correcting this injustice was Hitler's direct pretext for war. In March 1939, he demanded Poland return Danzig to Germany and allow highways to be built across the corridor

As Hitler drives triumphantly through the Sudetenland in 1938, taking it over, people along his route salute him. Is this Sudeten woman weeping tears of sorrow or joy?

to link greater Germany with its province of East Prussia. When Poland refused, Germany invaded. The reason given was the need to protect the German minority, who were being mistreated in Poland. Thus the principle of national self-government, conceived as a foundation for peace, was invoked as a rationale for war.

Mandates Override Self-Determination

Although self-determination was the guiding principle for drawing the borders in Europe, the Allies did not think it appropriate for other parts of the globe. Europeans had political experience, but other peoples were considered not sufficiently advanced to govern themselves. The populations of the now defunct Ottoman Empire in the Middle East and of the German colonies in Africa and the Pacific were in this category. What would their place be in the new world order?

Clemenceau and Lloyd George were adamant that the colonies not be returned to Germany. Wilson was equally adamant that they not be annexed to any Allied country. Yet they were not considered ready for self-rule. Some compromise was needed. Article XXII of the Covenant of the League of Nations established a form of government for these "peoples not yet able to stand by themselves." That form was the **mandate**.

A mandate was an order issued by the League of Nations to an "advanced" country giving that country the authority and responsibility to govern a "less advanced" country.

The less advanced country was called a mandate and the advanced country was a mandatory. The idea was for the mandatory to help and guide the mandates "until such time as they are able to stand alone." The League set up a commission to supervise the process.

The concept of the stronger nations helping the weaker ones grow into maturity sounds noble. However, World War I took place at the tail end of the Age of Imperialism, the time when European countries were competing to build empires. In 1914, there were five huge empires: Germany, Austria-Hungary, the Ottoman Empire, Russia, and the British Empire. The Allies looked at mandates not as opportunities

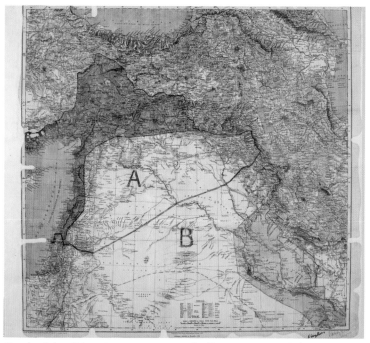

On the Sykes-Picot Agreement map, the line separating A from B divided what was to be French territory from what was to go to Britain. The yellow at bottom left is Palestine.

for development of self-government but as territories of people and resources to add to their domains.

The League set up three classes of mandates based on how long it might take for them to become independent states. Class A mandates could be expected to be self-governing relatively quickly. These were located in the former Ottoman Empire. Class B mandates needed considerably more time and oversight, whereas the Class Cs might never be able to stand on their own. The German colonies fell under Classes B and C. Several of the Allies had their eyes on potential mandates. Britain, France, Italy, Japan, Belgium, South Africa, Australia, and New Zealand all wanted something. How would the League decide who got what?

Secret Treaty Honored

In the case of the Ottoman territories, the decision had been made long before the peace conference even met. The empire was on the decline when it entered the war. It had been labeled the "sick man of Europe." Even if the Central Powers won the war, the Allies did not expect the Ottoman Empire to survive intact. Hoping the Allies would be victorious, diplomats from Britain and France began a series of meetings in 1915 to discuss what they thought should happen in the Middle East when the war was over.

What they thought, basically, was that the territory should be divided between their countries. Sir Mark Sykes of Britain and François Georges-Picot of France took out a map of the region and drew a line across it from east to west. Everything north of the line would go to France and everything south would go to Britain. They allotted a small area to Russia. The men signed their names at the bottom of the map and on an agreement they kept secret, tucked away until the empire was defeated.

The Sykes-Picot Agreement had to be kept secret because it conflicted with another, earlier arrangement. In fighting the Turks of the empire, Britain needed the help of the Arabs who lived in the region. If the Allies won with Arab help, Britain promised to secure an independent state for the Arabs. But the Sykes-Picot Agreement had no mention of an Arab state.

A second promise, made a year after the agreement, further complicated the matter. It was a response to **Zionism**, a movement of Jewish people to establish a homeland in Palestine. Some British politicians thought that supporting Zionism might entice neutral countries with sizable Jewish populations to get into the war on their side. British foreign secretary Arthur James Balfour wrote a letter to a Jewish leader in England ensuring him that the British government was favorable to "the establishment in Palestine of a national home for the Jewish people" and would do whatever it could to make that a reality. This became known as the Balfour Declaration. Jews worldwide saw it as a promise of a Jewish state in Palestine.

Thus, the delegates at the Paris Peace Conference were confronted with three contradictory promises regarding the same land. Jews thought it would be given to them, Arabs expected to rule it, and the British and French promised it to each other. Whatever solution was reached, someone was not going to be happy.

In the end, the secret Sykes-Picot Agreement was the basis of the settlement. The northwestern region of the empire had been allowed self-determination after it declared itself the Republic of Turkey. The remaining Ottoman territories were designated Class A mandates. France was made mandatory over Syria and Lebanon, and Britain had responsibility for Palestine and what is today Iraq. The lines that defined the different countries were drawn without regard for the many ethnic, cultural, language, and religious differences of the area. None of the inhabitants had a say in any of the decisions.

The British tried to appease the Arabs and Jews for not keeping their promises to them. They allowed Arabs to rule as kings over Iraq and Jordan, a country created in part of Palestine. They permitted a limited number of Jews to settle in the other part of Palestine. But there was no Arab or Jewish state; Britain remained firmly in control. As in Europe, the disappointment grew into bitterness and anger. And also as in Europe, the bitterness eventually erupted in violence. The process would take longer in the Middle East, but resistance to the European domination led to rebellions and war.

Secret Treaty Disregarded

The Sykes-Picot Agreement was not the only secret treaty with which the delegates in Paris had to deal. There was also the 1915 Treaty of London with Italy. Britain, France, and Russia had wanted Italy on their side in the war, but Italy was

ZIONISM

Of the many nationalistic movements of the late nineteenth and early twentieth centuries, one was Zionism. Named for a mountain in Jerusalem, Zionism was the term applied to a sentiment almost as old as the city. Ever since their exile in the first century from the land later called Palestine, the Jewish people had longed to return to their homeland.

The Zionist movement began to grow in 1896, when Theodor Herzl published *The Jewish State*. Herzl reminded his readers that no matter what country they were in or what language they spoke, Jews shared a common history and traditions. Therefore, the Jewish people were a nationality. He argued that as a nationality they should have a geographic and political identity–a Jewish state.

When Herzl wrote, Jews were scattered throughout many countries, with the majority in Eastern Europe and Russia. In some places they were persecuted as an unwanted ethnic and religious minority. These Jews welcomed Zionism as a cultural and religious movement.

However, at the turn of the twentieth century, not all Jews were persecuted. Many had assimilated into the cultures around them. Some no longer followed the Jewish customs or practiced the Jewish religion. Yet they were still Jewish. As they heard the growing cries of other nationalistic movements, they too began to feel a pride in their heritage. For them, Zionism was a secular and political cause leading inevitably to a geographic state.

That state could be located in only one place: Palestine. Palestine, the narrow strip of land between the Mediterranean Sea and the Jordan River, was the Jews' ancestral homeland. It was where their ancestor, Israel, had lived, the land they believed had been given to them by God. The goal of Zionism was the return of the Jewish people to their homeland in Palestine.

Many British leaders who held the mandate of Palestine agreed with and wanted to help the Jews. But Arabs were living in Palestine, and they also claimed that land. So the British admitted only a trickle of Jews into the mandate. After World War II, and the attempt to exterminate the Jews in the Holocaust, world opinion was sympathetic toward the Zionist movement. Britain, unable to work out an arrangement between Jews and Arabs, gave the mandate to the United Nations (UN), which had replaced the League of Nations. The UN divided Palestine into two states, one Arab and one Jewish, and made the city of Jerusalem a special district. However, the Arabs rejected the plan and civil war followed. The victorious Jews proclaimed the State of Israel in May 1948.

allied with the Central Powers. To lure Italy into their camp, the Allies promised it some of the land they hoped to win. Orlando came to the peace conference with the expectation of receiving that territory.

However, the other three of the Big Four did not want to honor Italy's legally valid claims. Clemenceau and Lloyd George were disappointed with the Italians' military performance and felt they had not lived up to their end of the bargain. Wilson argued that giving Italy all the land described in the treaty would violate the right of Serbians and Slavs to self-determination. Besides, he was against secret treaties and thought they need not be honored (even though he accepted the Sykes-Picot Agreement). Enraged, Orlando stormed out of the conference.

The Italian premier eventually returned, but Italy received only a tiny portion of the territory promised in the 1915 treaty. Orlando had been treated as a minor player in the negotiations and had been denied what was rightfully due his country. Italians condemned the settlement at Versailles as a "mutilated peace." Their lingering anger over the injustice was one of the forces Benito Mussolini tapped into to lead Italy to Germany's side in World War II.

Disarmament

Once the boundaries were settled, a major responsibility of the League of Nations according to its covenant was "the reduction of national armaments to the lowest point consistent with national safety." Wilson considered accomplishing this goal essential to maintaining peace. However, the League of Nations was slow to attend to this matter. Many League members were reluctant to disarm. France, ever concerned about possible German aggression, felt its arsenal of weapons was already too small. The newly formed European nations were also fearful of Germany, and they were uncertain anyone would come to their defense if attacked. Japan, beginning to flex its muscle and dream of empire, had no desire to give up any military strength. After some unproductive discussions, the League finally set up a commission in 1926 to prepare for a World Disarmament Conference scheduled for 1932 in Geneva, Switzerland.

Frustrated by the League's delays, the United States, which was not part of the association, decided to pursue Wilson's goal without the League. At the Washington Naval Conference in 1921, the US secretary of state succeeded in getting Britain and Japan to agree to limit the numbers of warships in their navies. In 1928, the US secretary of state and the French foreign minister authored the Kellogg-Briand Pact in which sixty-five nations renounced war as a means of solving their differences. But the agreement had no teeth; it did not specify what any of the sixty-five nations would do if threatened. Nor did it make any promises of reducing arms.

When the League's conference finally took place, it was a disaster. Germany was one of the sixty nations present, having been admitted to the League in 1926. Considering itself equal with all other countries at the meetings, Germany argued it should have the same level of weaponry as everyone else. That meant the Treaty of Versailles, which totally disarmed Germany, would need to be revised. France would never agree to such a demand. The German representatives walked out of the conference and soon withdrew from the League of Nations. The concept of worldwide disarmament was dead. The race to arm for the next war was on.

Easing of Reparations

At Versailles, France had pinned its hopes for permanent, or at least long-term, German disarmament on reparations. Clemenceau had tried to make the financial requirements so steep that Germany could not afford the weaponry needed to launch an effective military strike. His plan seemed to be succeeding, as Germany could not possibly pay the huge sums demanded.

The Reparation Commission allowed Germany to pay some of its reparations in kind—that is, in materials instead of currency. Germany was able to make payments in coal and timber, but production could not keep up with the payment schedule. Germany was continually defaulting, or failing to pay. In January 1923, France and Belgium sent soldiers into Germany to collect. For two and a half years, the soldiers occupied the Ruhr, the industrial area where most of Germany's coal and steel were produced.

The occupation of the Ruhr angered Germans, frustrated the Allies, and did little to solve the problem of Germany's

French troops march down a street in the German city of Dusseldorf in 1923. During the occupation of the Rhineland, scenes such as this were common.

inability to pay reparations. Germany was not trying to avoid its obligations. It was trying to meet them and so regain its standing as a respectable nation. The Allies realized that military action was not the answer. They came up with ways to help Germany rebuild its economy so it could pay the war debt on a reasonable timetable. Under the Dawes Plan, the Allies—primarily the United States—loaned Germany money. The Young Plan reduced the total amount due and set a new schedule for repayment.

Even with these adjustments, Germany fell farther and farther behind on its obligations. When the stock market crash of 1929 triggered worldwide economic depression, payment of reparations became a complete impossibility. US president Herbert Hoover called for and got a moratorium, or temporary halt, of reparations payments because of the financial crisis. Britain and France recognized the futility of requiring money that could not be paid and suspended all reparations at the 1932 Lausanne Conference. The next year Hitler became chancellor of Germany, and he canceled all German financial obligations, including loan repayments.

In these negotiations and deals, the United States played a major role, even though it was not part of the League of Nations or its Reparation Commission. Both the Dawes and Young Plans were arranged by US financial experts. America provided the bulk of the loans that helped all of Europe recover. The reason the United States could be so generous was that the war had changed global economic relations. The United States went into the war a debtor nation but emerged a creditor, having money to lend to and invest in other countries. The center of international finances moved from London to New York. America's new influence in world affairs meant that even though isolationist sentiments persisted, it could not afford to sit out World War II when it came.

LOST OPPORTUNITY

While the delegates at the Paris Peace Conference concentrated on preventing conflicts in Europe, they may have missed a chance to avert a twenty-year war that claimed the lives of more than three million people. That chance came in a petition presented to the Big Four by a group of men calling themselves "Annamite patriots."

Annam was the native word for a little-known Asian country then called French Indochina. It was a colony of France, and the native people chafed under foreign rule. The nationalistic fervor sweeping Eastern Europe was stirring hearts and minds in Asia as well. The Annamites were eager to free themselves from French domination.

Because they knew the French language, some from the colony had immigrated to France, where education and job prospects were better. Among them was a young man, almost thirty, going by the name of Nguyen Ai Quoc, "Nguyen the Patriot." He used a number of names, worked at a variety of jobs, and was given to exaggeration, so all the stories told of him may not be true. This much is known:

He spent his early twenties as a cook's helper on ships, traveling to Africa, Britain, and the United States before settling in France. In France, he joined the Socialist Party. He was part of the small group presenting his people's needs to the delegates at Versailles.

In the petition, the group appealed to the principle of national self-determination that recognized the "sacred right of all peoples to decide their own destiny." They asked that the principle be applied to the Annamite people.

If any of the Big Four read the petition, they did not respond. Rebuffed, Nguyen left the conference and turned to the French Communist Party. In 1941, he returned to his native land of French Indochina to lead an independence movement. He not only ousted the French, but also dealt the United States its first wartime defeat. He became president of what eventually became the independent nation of Vietnam. The last name he used was Ho Chi Minh, "Bringer of Light."

The League's Peacekeeping Record

Before the large-scale war began in 1939, smaller conflicts arose that threatened the peace secured at Versailles. The whole purpose of the League of Nations was to settle those differences before they grew into major clashes. The League's record at conflict resolution was mixed. The confrontation in the Ruhr demonstrated the problem the League encountered: it had no way to enforce its rulings. The United States was not a member, so its mighty army and economic power could not be brought to bear on a matter in which it chose not to be involved. In the first years, Britain had the only viable military force, and Britain did not want to police the world; it had enough problems keeping its colonies under control.

The League had a number of early successes. It settled a border dispute between Albania and Yugoslavia, coaxing Yugoslavian troops to withdraw. It resolved a controversy between Sweden and Finland over who should govern the Åland Islands. When Poles and Germans living in Upper Silesia were permitted to vote on which government they wanted to be under and the close vote resulted in violence, the League calmed the unrest by dividing the area in two. Bulgaria sought the League's help when invaded by Greece; the League convinced Greece to remove its armies and compensate Bulgaria for damages it had caused.

These were instances of the League fulfilling its mission: to prevent or settle conflicts. However, these were relatively minor disputes, and the affected countries were willing to

THE GAP IN THE BRIDGE.

This 1919 cartoon depicts the League of Nations as a bridge preventing countries from falling into the abyss of war. The United States, essential to the bridge, refuses to be part.

accept the League's decisions. When the countries were unwilling and the issues were larger, the League proved powerless to keep the peace.

An example is a disagreement between Poland and Lithuania. When the Allies established the border between the two countries, the city of Vilna fell within Lithuania. Historically, Vilna had been the capital of Lithuania, but the population of the city in 1920 was more Polish than Lithuanian, and Poland took Vilna by force. Lithuania appealed to the League and the League ruled that Poland should leave, but Poland refused. No League army came to force Poland to comply. Neither France nor Britain wanted to antagonize Poland; they needed a friendly country allied with them just in case Germany should strike again. So the violation stood.

The League was also silent when Poland invaded Russia in 1920. Poland did not have a disagreement with Russia; it simply wanted to enlarge its territory. Because France and Britain feared Russia and needed Poland, no one in the League protested. The League did not even try to stop the war.

In one very serious incident, a small party of Italians was murdered in Greece, and Italy demanded Greece execute the killers and pay a fine to Italy. Greece did not know who was responsible and refused to do anything. Italy then invaded and occupied the Greek island of Corfu. The League tried to diffuse the situation with a compromise. It condemned Italy but ordered Greece to pay the fine. Italy's leader, Benito Mussolini, objected, and the League gave in to his demands. Greece was made not only to pay the fine but also to pay it immediately and to apologize for the Italians' deaths.

As unsettling as the Corfu incident was, an even graver challenge to the League's ability to keep peace occurred in Asia. Japan staged an event to give it a pretext for invading the Chinese territory of Manchuria. No one intervened as Japan occupied Manchuria and set up a puppet state. The League condemned the action, but Japan ignored the reprimand. The League did not raise an army to free Manchuria and did not levy any economic sanctions against Japan.

It should be no surprise, then, that the League was totally ineffective when Italy sent its troops into Ethiopia (then Abyssinia) or when Germany and Italy supplied a rebellion in Spain with men and weapons. The League's impotence was obvious when Hitler defied the Treaty of Versailles by marching an army into the Rhineland and by merging Austria with Germany. The emperor of Ethiopia, Haile Selassie, warned that these failures to protect small states against strong aggressors threatened the "very existence of the League of Nations."

The emperor was right. The leaders of Germany, Italy, and Japan knew the League did not have the leaders, the power, or the will to oppose them. By the time Hitler crossed into Poland to begin World War II, the League was effectively dead and the Treaty of Versailles was null and void.

5

Peace in the Modern World

World leaders attempting to make World War I the war that ended wars did not fail completely. True, a second global war erupted and regional conflicts have taken place. However, the peacemakers of Versailles kept the world safe for twenty years. They accomplished this amid the collapse of an old order, the emergence of new nation-states, a worldwide depression, and widespread anger and resentment. That was no small achievement.

More importantly, some of the concepts of international relations they introduced took root and grew into policies and institutions that are in effect today. The principles of national self-determination, collective security, and mutual disarmament remained alive even though the organization that implemented them did not.

Opposite: US president Franklin Roosevelt (left) and British prime minister Winston Churchill (right) talk aboard the British battleship Prince of Wales, where they worked out the Atlantic Charter.

Once World War II began, the League of Nations was obviously irrelevant. It simply faded away, officially dissolving on April 18, 1946. In its place, a new association of countries was born. Its structures, purpose, goals, and membership were very similar to those of the League. However, its founders had reason to believe its success would be longer lasting. It had one critical element the League lacked: the participation of the United States.

The Atlantic Charter

When Woodrow Wilson published the United States' aims for the conclusion of World War I, the United States had not yet decided to enter the war. Similarly, in August 1941, almost two years into World War II, the United States was still neutral. Like Wilson, President Franklin Roosevelt was considering America's goals for the outcome of the conflict. Roosevelt consulted with British prime minister Winston Churchill and the two leaders developed their countries' proposal for the peace. They issued a joint declaration that became known as the Atlantic Charter.

As with Wilson's Fourteen Points, the Atlantic Charter was a statement of ideals the authors thought should be the basis of a just and lasting peace. Roosevelt and Churchill listed eight points. They retained the key principles that had been accepted into the Treaty of Versailles. After firmly renouncing any desire to gain territory for their own countries, they affirmed "the right of all peoples to choose the form of government under which they will live." In the new war, the Axis Powers of Germany, Italy, and Japan were forcibly taking over smaller nations, completely disregarding the wishes of their citizens. The first principle of the Atlantic Charter was the right of national self-determination, first enshrined as international policy in the Treaty of Versailles.

Two of Wilson's other ideals were also in the charter: unhindered trade and reduction of arms. Perhaps surprisingly, freedom of the seas found its way into the charter as well. This provision was one of the Fourteen Points Britain had vehemently rejected in 1919. In 1941, however, Churchill was willing to give in on this issue. He desperately wanted the United States to add its military might and its money to the Allied cause against the Axis aggression. If agreeing to free access to the world's waters was the price America wanted for joining the war, he would pay it.

In the emblem of the United Nations, a world map, with the North Pole rather than any nation at its center, signifies concern for all nations. The olive branches are symbols of peace.

Looking to the eventual end of the war and hoping for an end to all war, the Atlantic Charter held the same hope embodied in the League of Nations: collective security. The document called for collaboration between all nations in "the establishment of a wider and permanent system of general security."

Today's Association of Nations

The charter stopped short of suggesting exactly what that system of security should be. The joint declaration was a statement from two leaders only; a workable system of collective security would require many more partners. In 1941, it was impossible to predict who would win the war and which nations would come out intact. By 1944, prospects for an Allied victory appeared a little brighter, and Allied leaders began a series of meetings to discuss ways of maintaining peace. The result was the United Nations.

In some ways, the UN mirrored the League of Nations. Both organizations had a general assembly in which discussion took place, an executive council that made important decisions, and a secretariat that performed administrative functions. The name of the UN's executive council, the Security Council, reflects the association's emphasis on collective security in the wake of another world war.

Like the League's Executive Council, the UN Security Council is made up of permanent members and members who serve temporary terms. Again, like the League, the Council's permanent members are representatives from the countries that won the war: the United States, Britain, France, the Soviet Union, and China. Any of the five permanent members can veto any action of the other fourteen members. The UN is much larger than the League. It began in 1945 with 51 members and grew to 193 members by 2011.

The League of Nations had a number of commissions that performed humanitarian work. Among other activities, these groups returned prisoners of war to their home countries, fed and housed refugees, worked to eradicate certain diseases, and improved labor conditions in several nations. These efforts that promoted justice, health, and safety—especially for smaller, weaker, states—were seen as important in maintaining international peace and security.

The Charter of the United Nations built on these successes. The UN established a number of agencies dedicated to the health and well-being of people anywhere in the world, whether member nations or not. Many are better known by their acronyms (names formed by the letters of their formal names). UNESCO (the United Nations Educational, Scientific, and Cultural Organization) continues the work of the League's International Committee on Intellectual Cooperation. It provides a variety of literacy and teacher training programs, cultural projects, and human rights efforts. UNICEF (the United Nations Children's Fund) helps mothers and children in developing countries. The World Health Organization, World Food Program, World Bank, and other agencies provide assistance, education, research, and resources all over the globe.

Old Mandates, New Trusts

One piece of unfinished business the League of Nations left to the UN was the matter of mandated territories. In 1945, twelve mandates had not yet received independence. In addition, new lands fell to international supervision after World War II, including territories in the Pacific taken from Japan. Not wanting to use the term "mandate" because it made people think of the dependent lands as colonies, the UN replaced the mandate system with a trustee system. All the lands that were not self-governing were called "trusts." They were placed under the care of, or entrusted to, countries that would help them develop economically and politically.

Like the League, the UN based its system for managing the trust territories on the principle of national self-determination. Unlike the League, the UN maintained real oversight over the trustees and their trusts. A Trusteeship Council was one of the main structures of the United Nations. It was set up so that it included not only the trustee states but also an equal number of non-trustee nations. This made trustees accountable to a larger group and kept them from treating their trusts as colonies. It was a form of collective security for the trust territories.

The Trusteeship Council did not leave the decision of when a territory was ready for independence to the trustee; it sought input from the territories. It sent missions to the trusts regularly to monitor their development progress and the management of the trustees. It asked the trust territories

Police in the US trust territory of Palau greet a UN mission in 1973.
The center flag is the flag of the Trust Territory of the Pacific Islands.

to tell the Council when they thought they were ready to move forward.

Every trust did not become an independent state. Some, such as Alaska and Hawaii, elected to become part of the trustee nation. Independence itself was not the goal of the trustee system; self-determination was. Every UN trust territory freely and voluntarily chose its status. By 1994, there were no more trusts to oversee. One part of Wilson's dream, at least, had been achieved.

New Nationalism and Self-Government

Self-determination remained a political ideal for a long time. What had fueled the push for self-government at the end of World War I was the spirit of nationalism stirring in Europe, particularly in the Balkans. At the end of World War II, the

THE INTERNATIONAL LABOR ORGANIZATION

In its quest for a lasting peace, the Paris Peace Conference addressed the issue of labor. In the decades leading up to the war, workers' movements had provoked unrest throughout Europe, demanding decent treatment and higher living standards for working people. The delegates at Paris believed they could not sustain peace without social justice, which assured fair and equal opportunities for employment. They assigned the matter to a Labor Commission. The commission created an independent agency under the auspices of the League of Nations: the International Labor Organization (ILO). That organization, established by the Treaty of Versailles in 1919, has continued without interruption. Today it is a specialized agency of the United Nations, operating in more than 180 countries.

The purpose of the ILO has remained unchanged since its founding: to improve conditions for workers throughout the world. Its organizers realized they could not create policies and set standards for the workplace without hearing from people who were actually in the workplace, so they formed an organization that is unique among UN agencies. It is the UN's only tripartite agency—that is, its members represent three different groups: governments, employers, and workers. Representatives from each group have equal voice in the ILO's decisions.

In its first phase, under the League of Nations, the ILO defined minimum standards for the workplace and encouraged member nations to put those standards into law. During the Great Depression, the ILO instituted programs that put people back to work. As developing nations gained their independence, the ILO worked to raise wages and living standards and provide technical assistance.

The organization continually faces new challenges. It has successfully championed the rights and improved the lot of workers from the beginning of industry through the digital age. As a testimony to its success, the ILO was awarded the Nobel Peace Prize in 1969.

same spirit swept the colonies and trusts of Africa and the Pacific. In the decade and a half between the end of the war and 1960, thirty-seven new countries appeared in Africa, Asia, and the Middle East.

In Africa, nationalism was a product of **anti-colonialism**, the opposition to foreign rule. Whether they were called colonies or trusts, most parts of Africa were under the control of European powers after World War II. Even if the foreigners did not oppress the Africans, they exploited them. They used the labor and resources of their colonies for their own ends with little thought of self-government for the colonists. But under the watchful eye of the UN Trusteeship Council, the Europeans provided schools, jobs, and access to the political process.

Over time, the colonies prospered economically, and some inhabitants became doctors, lawyers, and other professionals. As they began to experience a little power, African colonists united in various types of groups—youth organizations, trade unions, and welfare associations—and pressed the colonial governments for reforms. Some of the groups grew into larger movements and the call for reform became a demand for independence. The pace and character of the movements differed by colony. In some places, the transition to self-rule was peaceful; in others, colonists were met with resistance and they resorted to arms. The nationalism in the colonies, known collectively as the African liberation movement, reached its peak in 1960. In that year alone, seventeen of the African territories won their independence and joined the United Nations.

*Fighters such as these of the Zimbabwe African National Liberation
Army took Rhodesia, a self-governing British colony in 1965, to
independence as the nation of Zimbabwe in 1980.*

While Africa was becoming liberated, much of Eastern
Europe was in the grip of the Soviet Union. Soviet troops that
had occupied territory during World War II simply remained
and exercised control over local governments, ruling them
as satellites. But nationalistic sentiments lay just beneath
the surface, ready to spring to life when the opportunity
presented itself. The opportunity came in 1989. The Soviet
leaders, suffering economically, relaxed some restrictions
on its satellites. The Solidarity movement of trade unions
in Poland took advantage of the softening and launched a
mostly peaceful revolution that freed that country. In a matter
of weeks, other Soviet-dominated countries followed suit—
Czechoslovakia, Romania, and the Baltic states. By 1990,
nationalism had restored self-government and redrawn the
map of Europe again.

Collective Security for New Kinds of War

The actions of the Soviet Union created a situation neither the League nor the United Nations could foresee: a cold war. The term "Cold War" refers to the period of tension between Western democracies, led by the United States, and Communist countries, led by the Soviet Union. The hostility stretched from the end of World War II until the breakup of the Soviet Union in 1990. It never became "hot," with actual shots fired, although at times it came close.

A cold war is basically a tense standoff. It is laced with suspicion, mired in mistrust and uncertainty. The two sides watch each other nervously, ready to strike should the other move. The only way to prevent a cold war from becoming hot is the threat that if one country attacks, several others are ready to counter; in other words, collective security. Collective security was the primary purpose of the United Nations. Members pledged to defend one another against aggression. The promise of mutual defense had not worked in the League because no nation enforced it. The UN could be expected to be more successful because it included all the countries with any military power to make or stop war.

However, one provision in the UN's charter limited its effectiveness in using that power: the veto privilege. Any single permanent member of the Security Council can veto any measure before the Council and the measure is defeated even if the other fourteen Council members and the entire General Assembly are in favor. During the Cold War, the United States exercised its veto privilege about sixty times, and the Soviet Union about eighty. More recently, in 2012, Russia's and China's vetoes kept the UN from intervening to end fighting and the killing of civilians in Syria. In October 2016, Russia vetoed a UN resolution calling for a halt to the bombing of Aleppo, Syria.

Because the UN could not provide adequate collective security, world leaders went back to an older method of defense. They formed multinational alliances rather than rely on an international association. In 1949, twelve nations of Europe and North America created the North Atlantic Treaty Organization (NATO), agreeing that an attack on any one of them would be treated as an attack on all. A similar organization, the Southeast Asia Treaty Organization

This aerial view of a missile launch site in Cuba shows the Soviet Union had removed its missiles that threatened the US. The 1962 Cuban missile crisis was a major Cold War showdown.

(SEATO), was founded in 1954. The Soviet Union entered into a mutual defense agreement with its satellites in Eastern Europe in 1955, known as the Warsaw Pact.

Arms Reduction

These alliances were leaders' attempts to ensure national security. To be secure, a country must have weapons, at least enough arms to defend itself. How many is enough? This has been the unanswered question since the League of Nations attempted to enforce international arms reduction. The issue is much more complex today than it was in 1919. The most sophisticated weaponry of World War I were tanks and rudimentary aircraft. Now leaders must consider not only highly advanced conventional armaments but also nuclear, chemical, and biological weapons. In addition, heavy weapons are no longer limited to the armies of nation states. Guerillas, terrorists, and other radical groups sometimes have access to large amounts of lethal arms.

Arms control has always been difficult. Probably the first attempt to limit weaponry was the Hague Convention of 1899. The treaty banned the use of poison gas, among other items. Despite the prohibition, poison gas was used fifteen years later in World War I. The League of Nations was never able to convince any country to limit its armaments.

Since those failures and continuing to today, there have been numerous discussions, conferences, and treaties attempting to ban or reduce the number of various

WORLD WAR II FINALLY ENDS ...
AFTER MORE THAN NINETY YEARS

After 1931, Germany did not owe any more reparations. Its war debt had been canceled. But in the 1920s, the country had borrowed money from foreign banks in an attempt to pay the enormous reparations. Hitler had declared all loans void, but Germany did not forget.

After Germany lost World War II, it was again in need of financial help. The chancellor of the new Germany, Konrad Adenauer, appealed to the world community. To show that his country could be trusted to repay all the money other nations would lend, Adenauer vowed to pay the outstanding amount from World War I. With interest.

When an agreement for repayment was reached in 1953, the chancellor asked for one condition. At that time Germany was actually two separate countries, the Federal Republic of Germany and East Germany. Hoping the two parts would one day be rejoined, Adenauer asked to postpone the interest payments until a unified Germany could pay them. No one expected the reunification to ever take place, but the creditor nations agreed anyway. They basically considered the interest debt forgiven.

By 1980, Germany had repaid the war debt. It rebuilt its economy and regained the trust and respect of other countries. Then, in 1990, to the surprise of the entire world, the Soviet Union disintegrated, and the two Germanys became one. True to its word, the new Germany formulated a plan to repay the interest on its World War I debt.

The plan called for twenty payments. On October 3, 2010, Germany made its final payment of 70 million euros ($94 million). Ninety-two years after the armistice silenced the weapons, World War I came to an end.

implements of war. There have been instances of international, multinational, regional, bilateral, and unilateral disarmament. Yet the UN estimated the cost of global military spending in 2010 at more than $1.5 trillion, and it is growing every year.

Today's leaders are facing the same realities League of Nations officials found; enforcement of the many agreements is a problem. In spite of the difficulties, they press ahead. They believe most people desire peace and they cannot have it in a world full of armaments. They believe arms reduction is an achievable goal, an ideal, and any progress toward achieving it is well worth the effort.

Legacy of Versailles

Perhaps that is the legacy of Versailles—the affirmation that ideals are worth striving for. When Woodrow Wilson outlined his Fourteen Points, many people considered them unrealistic. They sounded good, but most leaders doubted they could work in the real world. After the horror they had endured, the delegates to the Paris Peace Conference simply wanted to bring the bloody chapter to a close. They did not think that implementing specific principles might really make the world a safer place.

But Wilson persisted. He believed "a just and stable peace" could actually be secured "by removing the chief provocations to war." He insisted other world leaders consider those provocations—secret agreements, economic injustices, arms proliferation—and find ways to eliminate them. He believed everyone had the right to determine their own destinies, and he refused to allow powerful countries to ignore the rights of less powerful people. Wilson believed countries needed to join together, the strong with the weak, to ensure and preserve peace. He stubbornly held other leaders to the pursuit of that ideal.

The Treaty of Versailles incorporated a number of Wilson's principles. Instead of simply imposing a settlement, it established, in the Covenant of the League of Nations, a framework for peace that is in operation today. The leaders of the time were not completely successful in maintaining that peace, but they created structures and processes that future generations were able to use. In doggedly pursuing worthy ideals, the peacemakers gave the world the foundations for the peace we enjoy today.

annex To attach or add to something larger, making the annexed item part of the larger one.

anti-colonialism Opposition to control and rule of a dependent territory (colony).

armistice An agreement between warring parties to stop fighting temporarily, usually until a permanent peace treaty is agreed upon.

casualties In war, military people killed, missing, or wounded.

collective security A method of several countries ensuring the safety of one another by agreeing to act together when threatened.

demilitarized zone A geographic area in which no military personnel or weapons are allowed.

idealist A person whose attitudes and actions are based on thoughts of the way things should be, sometimes ignoring practical considerations.

indemnity Compensation or reimbursement for a loss. In the context of war and treaties, an indemnity is reimbursement the loser pays the winner for the costs the winner incurred in the war.

Irreconcilables The name given to a group of senators who refused to ratify the Treaty of Versailles under any circumstances.

isolationism An attitude, sometimes a policy, that a nation should not become involved in the affairs of other nations.

kaiser The title of the ruler of the German Empire from 1871 to 1918. Kaiser is the German form of "Caesar."

mandate An order from the League of Nations authorizing one of the Allies to govern a developing country; also the term for the developing country under the mandate.

nationalism Intense pride in and loyalty to one's nation.

occupation Physically taking over and controlling an area, usually by putting troops in an area.

ratify A vote to formally approve an item.

reparations Compensation paid by one party for damages that party inflicted on another.

self-determination The right of the people who live in a territory to decide what the form and practices of their government are.

sovereign Possessing complete power of self-government, free from any other ruler.

Zionism A movement of Jewish people in the late nineteenth and early twentieth centuries to establish a Jewish state in Palestine as their homeland.

1914-1918 World War I is fought between Central Powers and Entente (Allies).

1915, April 16 Italy signs Treaty of London, joining Allied side in war in return for promise of territory.

1916, May 19 Britain and France sign the Sykes-Picot Agreement, dividing the territory of the Ottoman Empire between them.

1917, April 6 United States enters World War I as an Associated Power on the side of the Allies.

1917, December 6 Russia signs armistice with Germany.

1918, January 8 Woodrow Wilson announces his Fourteen Points in a speech to the US Congress.

1918, November 11 Germany and Allies sign armistice ending World War I.

1919, January 18–January 21, 1920 Paris Peace Conference writes the Treaty of Versailles, including the Covenant of the League of Nations.

1919, February 14 Wilson presents draft of Covenant of the League of Nations to plenary session of Paris Peace Conference. Wilson departs conference to present plan to US Congress.

1919, February 28 Wilson presents draft of Covenant of the League of Nations to US Congress.

1919, May 7 Germany is presented with the Treaty of Versailles.

1919, June 28 Germany and Allies sign the Treaty of Versailles.

1919, September 3–October 2 Wilson campaigns in United States for ratification of treaty.

1919, November 19 US Senate rejects Treaty of Versailles. Senate rejects treaty a second time on March 19, 1920.

1919, July 2 Knox-Porter Resolution officially ends US war with Germany.

1920, January 10 The Treaty of Versailles goes into effect, simultaneously inaugurating the League of Nations.

1922 France and Belgium occupy Ruhr.

1926 Germany is admitted to the League of Nations.

1932–1933 World Disarmament Conference fails to reach agreement and Germany withdraws from League of Nations.

1939, September 1 Germany invades Poland, beginning World War II.

1945, October 24 Charter of the United Nations is ratified.

Books

Mee, Charles L., Jr. *Versailles: The End of the War to End All Wars.*
Boston, MA: New World City, 2014.

Neiberg, Michael S. *The Treaty of Versailles: A Concise History.*
New York: Oxford University Press, 2017.

Shepley, Nick. *The Paris Peace Conference 1919: A Student's Guide
to the Treaty of Versailles.* Luton, UK: Andrews UK Limited, 1015.

Websites

A Multimedia History of World War I

http://www.firstworldwar.com

This easily searchable and easy-to-navigate website contains a wealth of general information on every aspect of the war, including many primary source documents.

International Encyclopedia of the First World War

http://encyclopedia.1914-1918-online.net

A reference for World War I, this online encyclopedia contains a timeline and articles arranged by theme and region of the conflict.

US Department of State: Office of the Historian

https://history.state.gov

This website gives the history of US foreign relations. Under "Key Milestones," it has information about US involvement in world affairs by historic period.

Videos

The Peacemakers

https://www.youtube.com/watch?v=74-HkCRozls

This BBC documentary gives an in-depth look at people, process, and impact of the Treaty of Versailles.

The Treaty of Versailles in 1919 and Its Consequences

https://www.youtube.com/watch?v=KfnEy8FuElc

This video discusses the intricacies of the treaty and the aftermath of its signing.

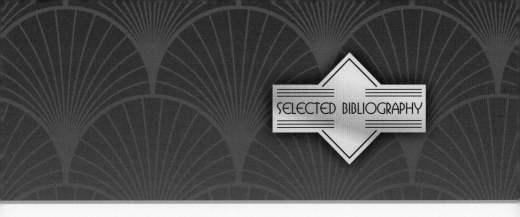

Anderson, Scott. "The True Story of Lawrence of Arabia."
Smithsonian Magazine, July 2014. http://www.
smithsonianmag.com/history/true-story-lawrence-arabia-
180951857/?spMailingID=21097645&spJobID=360468626
&page=1&spReportId=MzYwNDY4NjI2S0&spUserID=NzQwN
DU1MDM1MDIS1.

Beck, Sanderson. *World Peace Efforts Since Gandhi: History
of Peace, vol. 2*. Santa Barbara, CA: World Peace
Communications.

Current History (monthly magazine of *New York Times*) vol. 10,
April 1919–September 1919. https://books.google.com/
books?id=WLMqAAAAYAAJ&pg=PA192-IA15&lpg=PA192-IA
15&dq=Dr+Hermann+Mueller+and+Dr+Johannes+Bel
l&source=bl&ots=9ZGcaREHxO&sig=LP_0BDTdTivmDuX
GE2GYzKCefDc&hl=en&sa=X&ved=0ahUKEwif7dO4o4_
QAhUKw1QKHQJ3B9sQ6AEIUzAO#v=
onepage&q&f=false.

Grossman, Richard S. *Wrong: Nine Economic Policy Disasters and What We Can Learn from Them.* New York: Oxford University Press, 2013.

Hankey, Lord. *The Supreme Control at the Paris Peace Conference 1919: A Commentary.* New York: Routledge, 2015.

International Labor Organization. "Origin and History." http://www.ilo.org/global/about-the-ilo/history/lang--en/index.htm.

MacMillan, Margaret. "Lessons from History: The Paris Peace Conference of 1919." *Global Affairs Canada*, April 25, 2013. http://www.international.gc.ca/odskelton/macmillan.aspx?lang=eng.

——. *Paris 1919: Six Months that Changed the World.* New York: Random House, 2003.

Simpkin, John. "French Property Loses: 1914–1919." *Spartacus Educational*, updated August 2014. http://spartacus-educational.com/FWWproperty.htm.

Storey, William Kelleher. *The First World War: A Concise Global History.* Lanham, MD: Rowman and Littlefield, 2009.

United Nations. "Disarmament." http://www.un.org/en/globalissues/disarmament.

INDEX

Ann Byers is a teacher, youth worker, writer, and editor with a passion for history. In addition to studies of American and world history, she has written nine books on the Holocaust. This is her second book on the period between the world wars.